Familial
Undercurrents

Afsaneh Najmabadi

Familial Undercurrents

UNTOLD STORIES OF LOVE AND MARRIAGE IN MODERN IRAN

Duke University Press   Durham and London   2022

© 2022 Duke University Press
All rights reserved
Printed in the United States of America on acid-free paper ∞
Designed by A. Mattson Gallagher
Typeset in Garamond Premier Pro by Copperline Book Services

Library of Congress Cataloging-in-Publication Data
Names: Najmabadi, Afsaneh, [date] author.
Title: Familial undercurrents : untold stories of love and marriage
in modern Iran / Afsaneh Najmabadi.
Description: Durham : Duke University Press, 2022. |
Includes bibliographical references and index.
Identifiers: LCCN 2021020918 (print)
LCCN 2021020919 (ebook)
ISBN 9781478015154 (hardcover)
ISBN 9781478017776 (paperback)
ISBN 9781478022398 (ebook)
Subjects: LCSH: Najmabadi, Afsaneh, 1946—Family. |
Marriage—Iran—History—20th century. | Families—
Iran—History—20th century. | Families—Iran—History—
20th century—Case studies. | Marriage—Iran—History—20th
century—Case studies. | BISAC: HISTORY / Middle East /
Iran | SOCIAL SCIENCE / Ethnic Studies / American /
Native American Studies
Classification: LCC HQ666.4 .N356 2022 (print) |
LCC HQ666.4 (ebook) | DDC 306.810955/0904—dc23
LC record available at https://lccn.loc.gov/2021020918
LC ebook record available at https://lccn.loc.gov/2021020919

Cover art: *Four generations*, 12 May 1936. Author family photo.
Courtesy the Women's Worlds in Qajar Iran archive, Harvard
University.

For Bushra and Naseem

CONTENTS

CAST OF CHARACTERS

'Abbas	*my father*
'Alaviyeh Khanum (Khanum jun)	*my maternal grandmother*
Aqa'i	*my paternal grandfather*
Aqa jun	*Nuri Khanum's father*
Badi' al-Saltaneh	*my maternal grandfather*
Badi' al-Muluk	*my aunt*
Fakhr al-Muluk	*my aunt*
Fari	*my mother*
Gawhar al-Muluk	*my aunt*
'Iffat Khanum	*my aunt*
'Isa Khan	*'Iffat's husband and 'Abbas's uncle*
Latifeh Khanum	*my aunt*
Mansureh Khanum	*my father's other wife*
Nuri Khanum	*my paternal grandmother*
Qamar al-Muluk	*my cousin*
Sadiqeh Khanum	*Nuri's sister*

This book is inspired by a personal story. In early March 1987, I received a phone call from Tehran. On the other side of a bad connection, a man claimed he was my brother-in-law, married to my sister Mina. I had never before known of a sister named Mina. This was a short few months after my father's death in October 1986 (in Cambridge, Massachusetts). Rather shocked, I asked him to send me any corroborating documents, discontinued the conversation, and conveniently tucked it away into forgetfulness. I disbelieved the claim, and for a combination of reasons (including my mother's distress and refusal to meet with them on her visits to Iran), I did not connect with Mina until twenty years later. In 2005, I began to visit Iran regularly. I met Mina for the first time in 2007; slowly and hesitantly, I established a relationship with her. But then I became gripped with a detective fever, with an obsession to know about my father's other life, the family he had kept a secret from us.

Over the following years, I interviewed numerous people on Mina's mother's side of the family, my father's side of the family, and my mother's as well. A much more complicated and fascinating family story emerged from these conversations as I learned the story of this "other family" I had to trace, and retrace, many times over. I would find a new piece of information that would splice together previously disconnected episodes. At the same time, filling those gaps would push apart other episodes I thought had fit together. Smoothing one set of edges would frustratingly create other ragged ones that would refuse to fit. The second family turned out to include a first love and many unexpected turns and twists. Over the many years that I followed these conversations, the stories often changed from one telling to another. At the end, a relatively coherent story (for the most part!) took shape.

Mina's mother, Mansureh, had had a roughly sixth-grade formal education. In subsequent years (in the mid-1930s), she had been tutored in literary and religious texts by my father's father. Apparently, he had tutored several members of Mansureh's family, and socialized with them, all the way to the end of his life in 1948. Mansureh was possibly also tutored in math by my father, 'Abbas. That is how they met. My father fell in love with her and asked for her hand in marriage. Apparently, Mansureh was also fond of my father. Her mother, however, opposed the marriage—she had already promised her daughter to her brother's son, who was also very much in love with Mansureh. My paternal grandfather, Aqa'i, had also been very fond of Mansureh. I was told by Mina's husband that, at one point, my grandfather even considered transferring the title deed of his house to her name.

This was rather unusual. Was this reported intention meant to support the veracity of the "first love" story? Why would he transfer his property? To persuade Mansureh's mother to let his son marry her daughter? But then one would expect him to turn the ownership to 'Abbas, as it was done in numerous marriage contracts. Usually, part of the *mahr* included property that belonged to the groom's father, and then the groom's father would turn that property over to the groom, but never to the bride. In any case, if that was the intention, it failed. Mansureh and her cousin were contractually married (*'aqd*) on 26 May 1936. However, their marriage was not consummated for another six years, in October 1942, at which point Mansureh renegotiated her mahr, increasing it from 8,000 to 60,000 rials.

Six years was a rather long period between signing the marriage contract and its consummation. That too was unusual. A time lapse between the formal marriage contract and the wedding was not unusual. But it usually lasted between a few months or at most a couple of years; sometimes the bride was considered not physically mature enough for consummation of marriage, or sometimes the groom needed the time to prepare properly for his wife-to-be. But six years was highly unusual.

For a couple of years, Mansureh's husband had been away on his military service. But then, how to explain the other four years? Was Mansureh resisting the wedding, hoping her cousin would release her from the marriage contract? In the meantime, in September 1941, my father, 'Abbas, had met my mother, Fari, fallen in love with her, and married her in January 1942. Was that why Mansureh eventually resigned herself to the marriage with her cousin in October 1942? Fari and Mansureh had two daughters in exactly the same years, 1944 and 1946. Throughout the 1940s, both 'Abbas and his father had continued to visit Mansureh. She was apparently unhappy with her marriage. Her husband was a member of the Tudeh Party; he couldn't hold a steady job and would be fired frequently for his labor organizing. Money was not an issue, since he had inherited much property near Tehran. But apparently the unsettled pattern of life was unbearable for Mansureh. In 1947, she asked for her full mahr to be paid, presumably hoping to bargain it back in exchange for a divorce. Her husband turned over all his properties to her but refused to divorce her for another five years. By all family accounts, this was because he had been so in love with her that he wouldn't give up hope for a possible reconciliation. In the meantime, 'Abbas had purchased a piece of land in September 1948, close to where Mansureh had been living, built a house on it, and turned the house to Mansureh in the spring of 1949. This enabled her to move out of her marital home and live with her children in the new house, which she shared with her mother and for a few years with her grandmother as well.

Mansureh remained on friendly terms with her cousin even after the divorce and her marriage to 'Abbas; her now-ex-husband visited the girls frequently. Once Mina was born, he was very kind and fatherly to her as well. Mina recalled fondly some of the gifts that he had brought her, including a first camera.

In effect, not only had my father kept two families through the legal possibility of bigamy, but Mansureh too had two men in her life from the mid-1930s to the time of her cousin's death in 1980. One was her husband, the other, a family friend; by the early 1950s, they switched positions. The cousin/ex-husband continued to visit the family as a friend. Mansureh had managed to keep the two men openly as family; my father chose to hide one family from the other. This, at first, seems quite counterintuitive—that the woman seemed to have had more leeway than the man!

During these years of playing family detective, I also started talking about my family story to anyone willing to listen. In almost every instance, the response was something like, "Oh, yes, so-and-so in my family acted similarly. Only after his death we learned he had another wife." The repetition of the pattern made it clear that my father's secret family was not simply a quirky exception. It seems that over a short generation, what had been an acceptable open practice—men's polygyny—had become, for at least a layer of urban, educated, middle-class Iranian men, something socially frowned upon; it was something to keep secret, even though it was not illegal. After all, my mother had grown up in a bigamous household. While my father's father had married only once, numerous men in the larger Najmabadi clan of his father's generation had more than one wife.

Beyond my personal family fever, I thus became preoccupied with understanding this larger pattern of change in familial practices. This book aims at a historical contextualization of the changes in ideas of what constituted a family, how these changes came about, and how practices of family life adapted—or did not. Its scope is limited to Tehran and its newly emerging middle class in the middle decades of the twentieth century. Whether further generalizations could be made remains a topic for future research.

In the first chapter, "Marrying for Love," I trace how this idea entered and acquired dominance within a layer of the urban middle class, especially for women who also expected the companionate marriage to be monogamous. I look at how the diverse literature of the late nineteenth into the early twentieth century contributed to this process. In particular, I discuss romantic novels and morality tales, reformist newspapers, works of satire, plays, writings about social life in Europe, and somewhat later romantic films.

The second chapter, "Objects," presents ordinary objects of everyday life in terms of how they contributed to conjugalization of the family. These include letters of affection, exchanged at times between a man and a woman who had married contractually ('aqd) but had not yet cohabited; wedding outfits that marked the new couple from their parents' generation; wedding studio photographs; and more generally family photographs that contributed to and at the same time resisted conjugalization of the family.

"Meanings of Marriage," the third chapter, takes up the changes from the older concept of what forming a family was for (forming a household and begetting children) to the couple-centered family of the modern period. Concurrently, the practice of *mut'a* (*sigheh*)—a marriage for a fixed period of time—for (male) sexual pleasure became reconceptualized as religiously sanctioned prostitution. For more modernized men, sigheh was replaced by taking a *maîtresse* (mistress). Other men practiced sigheh both secretly and openly. The chapter also considers how women reacted to finding out that their husbands had taken another wife.

The last chapter, "Urban Transformations," analyzes how the growth of cities enabled having two families in one city, one unknown to the other. Keeping a secret family depended on the rupture of networks of information and gossip within a small neighborhood. These transformations also changed the size and architecture of houses, which were no longer suitable for keeping two wives in one household. The smaller housing units became couple-centered, even if at times one of the in-laws lived with the couple. Lastly, the epilogue brings out how these changes have changed the naming of marriage and of kin.

Much of the material for this study comes from the life stories that people told me in these years of interviews. At the time of these interviews and conversations, I had no plan to write a book. With no prior permission, I have thus changed names and other identificatory markers. My parents' story became one of them. Integrating my family story into the narrative of all the chapters has meant that I also have become a character in this text.

I wove the stories I heard with archival material to trace the transformation of concepts and practices of what constitutes family. I also use material objects of everyday life—photographs, clothes, letters written by couples, among other things—to trace how this change took shape. This latter body of archives became available to me through working on Women's Worlds in Qajar Iran. Some of the challenges of using this archive to write this manuscript I discuss in "In Lieu of an Introduction." Further, I discuss the ethics of telling stories that people seemed not to want to tell, as well as the issues of writing a manuscript in which I appear both as a character and as a historian.

ACKNOWLEDGMENTS

Started in 2014, this book has accumulated much debt over the years of its writing and many rewritings. During these years, I have enormously benefited from conversations and correspondence with many colleagues, friends, and family, and it is my pleasure to thank them here: Suad Joseph, Laura Wexler, Lila Abu-Lughod, Deniz Kandiyoti, Sue Lanser, Jill Lepore, Irvin Schick, Naghmeh Sohrabi, Naseem Makiya, Bushra Makiya, Kanan Makiya, Judith Surkis, Janaki Nair and the Feminist Faculty Collective at Jawaharlal Nehru University, Farshideh Mirbaghdadabadi, Azadeh Tajpour, Heather Love, Mana Kia, Houchang Chehabi, Amy Motlagh, Jaleh Jalili, Pamela Karimi, and Talinn Grigor. Also, special gratitude to Michael M. J. Fischer, to whom I owe not just many insights but also the title of this book.

Various parts of the book were presented at Rutgers University, the University of Pennsylvania, Columbia University, and Jawaharlal Nehru University. In each instance, I received invaluable feedback from the audience.

Several grants from Harvard University supported the research and writing of this book. I am deeply grateful for a grant from the Anne and Jim Rothenberg Fund for Humanities Research, to Peter Marsden in his capacity at the time as dean of social science, and to Michael Smith in his capacity at the time as dean of the Faculty of Arts and Sciences.

I had great research help from Huma Utku, Monique Hassel, and Reza Salami and transcription help from Shahrad Shahvand. I thank Emma Dolkhanian for helping me with deciphering and typing up my mother's written memoirs.

The writing of this book took an unusual detour. In late March 2017, I was diagnosed with cancer, and the next six months, taken up with ensuing treatment, gave me a break from a tightly scheduled life, which had been intended to enable me to complete a first draft during my 2016–2017 academic leave. My recovery turned out to be a gift of reflective incubation for this project, especially as it coincided with my immersion in reading the doctoral dissertation of Michael Amico, "The Forgotten Union of the Two Henrys." More than any other previous attempt (and the wonderful feedback I had received with each rewrite), Amico's work impacted my final decisions on how to rewrite this text. Years of sustained conversations with Mike, even before I imagined writing this book, throughout its shaping, writing, and rewritings, have seeped in, in numerous ways, within the veins of this book. Perhaps the traces are visible just to him and me. Being grateful goes nowhere close to saying something about my deep debt to these conversations, but grateful I am.

I am also thankful for suggestions from the anonymous readers of the manuscript.

Last but not least, I would like to thank my superb editor at Duke University Press, Courtney Berger, whose suggestions for revision were of enormous help.

In Lieu of an Introduction

From the outset, this project took shape under the shadow of two major challenges that affected the structure of writing and the approach to sources and their uses. In simplest form, these challenges were as follows:

> *How to think about the ethics of telling stories that people did*
> *not want re-told*
> *How to tell a story in which I was implicated both as a character*
> *and as a historian*

How to Think about the Ethics of Telling Stories That People Did Not Want Re-told

My mother chose not to talk about my father's second marriage with anyone beyond a couple of her siblings and nieces. Nor did she even hint at it in her interviews in the 1990s and in her written memoirs. My father had kept his second family a secret from the first to his dying days.

Their silence posed for me, throughout the work on this project, the unresolvable ethical dilemma that many (auto)biography writers and memoirists have noted. As Nancy Miller has put it, "Memoir writers necessarily blur the lines between autobiography and biography, self and other, especially when a child tells the parents' story." Telling these stories is "to retrieve a past that is ours but not ours alone."[1]

What right did I have to write my parents' story when they had chosen silence? Shouldn't I respect my father's secrecy and my mother's desire for keeping its knowledge confined? I understood my father's keeping the second marriage a secret to have been an effect of a middle-class modernist and Baha'i embarrassment, if not shame, over his bigamy, his way of living his love for Mansureh under circumstances that had made that option no longer a publicly accepted practice. As Deborah Cohen has put it in a different context, "Secrecy guaranteed both security and authenticity."[2] In my father's case, the authenticity of his being a modern Baha'i, whose new faith emphasized monogamy much more strongly than his old faith and practices in his parental generation had, and security from the possibility of losing Fari and the custody of his two children (me and my sister, Farzaneh), a possibility that had been shaped by my mother's education and professional life, as well as the support she received from her family (inclusive of her sister's husband who was my father's uncle too)—secrecy guaranteed both.

I understood my mother's desire for keeping a relative silence over that belated knowledge as her way of saving face, of remaining respectful as many relatives had said, in circumstances where things going wrong in marriage were by default seen as shortcomings of the wife. But things mattered only if they were known. Keeping silent made keeping face possible. I thus justified my desire to tell their story as my way of attempting to open up the possibility of reducing injury and disrespect, embarrassment and shame, over their life choices.

It is at times said that historians are motivated by the desire to speak of the dead and, even more, to speak on behalf of the dead. Some of the recent decades of recuperative historiography have indeed been informed by this desire to compensate for silences in history and give voice to the silenced. Yet what of the desire of the dead to remain silent? What of the lives made possible through keeping silent?

Quite early on, when I first started thinking about this project, I contacted one of my maternal cousins to inquire about memories of our mothers and our grandmother. She was reluctant to talk; she wrote that her "first reaction was that I wanted to 'protect' them and their legacy. Would my mother or yours want to have the public exposed to the 'family secrets'?" What right did I have, she insisted, to tell the stories of "family members unable to speak for themselves"?

At the time, I shrugged this objection off, largely because I was thinking of my writing as an act of empathy with these lives, not as critical judgment of their choices, decisions, and lives lived. As my work developed, I was even more certain that I could write in total empathy with all my characters; though at times empathy with my father would become challenging!

Nonetheless, my cousin's early warning remained an echo in my head that wouldn't go away. Conversations with other relatives would bring it back in new contexts. A paternal uncle talked about several incidents he had heard about: two related to my father's "scandalous behavior," apparently propositioning other women from the family, but several were about other people — so many Najmabadi men's scandals . . . we began to joke about whether this was a genetic trait! Each time, he made it clear that none of these stories were meant for re-telling. He emphasized that even though he talked about these stories to me, this had been a very rare thing for him to do; he definitely would not want any story to be re-told. Another relative told similar stories about Najmabadi men, repeatedly prefacing each story by saying, "I don't engage in gossip, *astaghfar allah* [may God forgive me], but . . ."

The repeated disavowal of gossip, in conversations with Arafat Razzaque and his dissertation on ethics of speech in the formation of early Islamic piety, brought forth another layer of this shadowy weight on my writing.[3] I too had grown up within an ethics of speech centered on restraint of the tongue, *hifz al-lisan*. This ethics was not simply located within the high Islamic culture of texts and teachings on piety, within books of ethics and injunctions to the pious. I too had grown up with cautions concerning excesses of talking that seeped through often-repeated advice: Why do you think God has given you two ears and one tongue? Hear twice before you talk once.

Most severely, the narrative attributed to the Prophet on gossip was often repeated: *al-ghiba ashaddu min al-zina*, roughly translated as "gossip is worse than fornication." Given that telling about someone else's sinful deed is considered a sin, and perhaps even a more severe sin than the committing of the sin itself, how does one go about telling other people's lives — sins and all? Given the culture of keeping things unsaid, letting things pass rather than be told and re-told, how ethical is my writing of other people's stories? If we take gossip itself as a critical "way of knowing," indeed, at times, as a "weapon of the weak," as an important source for historical cultural understanding, how do we deal with the shadow of shame hanging over the knowledge generated through gossip?

Within this kind of cultural ethos, how does one write about family secrets in a way that does not do harm to others' sensibilities? Is there a way of telling a story they had chosen not to tell that would open up possibilities of reducing injury and disrespect? Do I just not tell things that were "too scandalous"? Clearly my father didn't want the family on this side of town to know about the family on the other side of town. His story had, of course, already come out after his death because of legal requirements related to inheritance division, but even then, it had remained known only within a limited circle of people. Yet over the past years, my pursuit of his story has made it known to ever wider circles of people. Each time when I started a conversation with another relative by saying, "Did you know my father had another wife?," I made that circle of knowing larger. Writing and publishing a book would make it known to an even wider circle.

The ethics and politics of retrieving a past "that is not ours alone" is not simply a memoirist's dilemma, of course. This is what historians do all the time. Usually, we have no reason to assume that the stories retrieved are objectionable to those whose stories we have retrieved. But we also usually have no information on whether it would *not* be objectionable. For characters unknown to us personally, we tend not to worry.

What are the ethics of using what we save, or have been entrusted to keep? My parents had come to London in the winter of 1980 to visit me and my family. They had planned to stay a month or so, then go to Phoenix, Arizona, to visit my sister. The visit became an immigration: we insisted that they were retired and both their children were abroad; life in Iran, especially in the middle of nowhere on the outskirts of a small town, during the early revolutionary years of upheaval and with attacks against Baha'is, seemed to be too risky to return to, even though my father's conversion might not have been locally known. Why not stay for a while in the United States until things calmed down? We kept them abroad.

They had come with two suitcases. The following spring, on my visit to Tehran, I selected things to bring for them: some clothes, a few books, a selection of photographs from family albums, and a bunch of letters tied together. I recognized my father's handwriting. On closer inspection, they turned out to be letters my father had written over the first year of my parents' marriage when he was not in Tehran with his new bride. These also came with me. At one point, when my mother was angry at my father after she had found out about his other wife, she had wanted to throw them out. I told her I would like to save them; they became mine, though I did not read them until my familial detective journey began in 2014.

Is it ethical to use my father's letters to my mother, which she wanted to throw out? Just because I asked her to let me keep them and she agreed? At the time, of course, neither she nor I had any reason to imagine that some two decades later I would be writing this manuscript. What makes them mine to use for this project?

Nor is it just a problem in relation to my own family history. Since 2009, I have worked on Women's Worlds in Qajar Iran (wwQI), a digital archive and website. We visit families to photograph and digitize their relevant documents, photographs, and objects of daily life. Within that context, I have heard numerous stories of lives. A photograph brings out a memory, an object becomes the occasion for recalling a relative's wedding, yet another family story. When families have agreed, we have recorded these stories and the audio files are available to the public. Some stories, we were explicitly told, were not for public use. We either did not tape them or else kept them unpublished. But I, as the writer of these lines, have heard them; there is no way of erasing them from my mind. Invariably these stories have impacted how I understood other documents and objects from their family and have also influenced my thinking about other people's lives. At times, I have changed names and details in order to use a family vignette. Is that an ethical use of stories I heard?

There is a similar problem in relation to my conversations with my own relatives. This was not a structured ethnographical project. When I began to visit and speak with many relatives in pursuit of understanding my parents' life and my father's other family, I had no plan or thought of writing a book. I just wanted to know, especially to know my father who had suddenly become an enigmatic character for me. I thus did not seek formal permission for what I might, in some future date, do with what I heard. I did not tape these conversations. Often at the end of the day, recalling the conversations and writing about them was my way of reflecting over my parents' lives. When I decided there was a story worth telling, only then did I begin to take more formal notes and tape some of the conversations. Again, I have changed names, relations, and details. But is it ethical to use stories told by people who had no idea, nor did I, that their stories could be re-told in writing?

The privileged access I have had to one family's papers extends decades before the WWQI project, or any imagined manuscript I would be writing, further complicating the issue of the use of such papers in subsequent research. In 1992, I had edited and published an 1894 (previously unpublished) manuscript by Bibi Astarabadi, *Ma'ayib al-rijal* (Vices of men); in winter 1994, I received a letter from one of her granddaughters, Mihrangiz Mallah. Thus began my correspondence with her, which subsequently developed into visiting the family. Mihrangiz said that she had prepared the life narrative of her mother (Afzal) and wished to publish it. Several years before Afzal passed away in 1980, one of her sons, Husayn'ali Mallah, had recorded an extensive interview with her about her life. A few years after her death, upon her brother's suggestion, Mihrangiz had transcribed the interview. She had then prepared a narrative of her mother's life, based on the transcript and other family information, but composed as if in Afzal's voice. She inquired if I was interested to help with its publication. I was, of course, delighted. I asked whether the original tapes were available. They were not; after their transcription, the tapes had been reused for new recordings (very common in Iran at the time, given the price of cassette tapes and a dominant recycling culture). I requested a copy of the full transcription (upon which her ventriloquized manuscript had been based). This came months later (in July 1997), after her book had been published. I read it immediately and was taken aback by how much had been removed or radically changed and how much had been added into the published text that was not there. I found the original interview transcription immensely more powerful and felt that it had been a pity to have transformed it into a different text.

Soon, one of Mihrangiz's nieces contacted me and expressed interest in translating her aunt's book into English. Giving a couple of examples from the transcription, I asked Mihrangiz if we could add sections from the transcript into the English translation. She declined, feeling that such inclusion would upset her consideration of keeping everyone satisfied. She did not wish to write things that would cast life in Mazandaran (much of her mother's interview had been centered on her life there) in a negative light.[4] The English translation was not published; decades later the transcription was digitized and added to the Mahlaqa Mallah collection on the wwqi site.[5] By then Mihrangiz had passed away and there was no way of knowing if she would have given her permission for this inclusion.

Knowing Mihrangiz's earlier reluctance, was it ethical on my part to push for that inclusion — thus making it available worldwide? Was this interview transcript hers? Her brother's? Her mother's? I could tell myself that this was an anticensorship measure, given how much Mihrangiz had changed her mother's account in the first place. Yet I cannot stop thinking that my insistence must have had something to do with the fact that the shift within one generation in narratives about familial life, as evidenced in a comparison of the transcription and the published text, aligned with my thinking about changes in concepts and practices of marriage and family so perfectly as to make its broader availability to historians irresistible.

How to Tell a Story in Which I Was Implicated
Both as a Character and as a Historian

The second dilemma posed the difficult question of the structure of the text. This manuscript went through many more reconceptualizations and rewritings than any of my previous writings, and still I had no really satisfactory resolution for its structure. Should I tell the story as a continuous narrative, not burdened with historical contextualization of a historian, or is such contextualization unavoidable and critical to the very telling of the story itself? Should I tell the story, followed by a series of historical essays, so that readers with varying interests could select what they read? How much of myself as a family member as well as a family detective and my sleuthing footprints do I preserve in the telling of the story, without overwhelming the story with an authorial I? Both as a character within the story and as a historian, I became engaged in detective work. As one question seemed to come close to an answer, numerous new puzzles would emerge. How would I keep the traces of personal and historical detective work, which is what makes research exciting, without overwhelming the story itself?

Like a real-life crime detective, like a good investigative reporter, a historian – cum – family detective needs a frame, "a loose frame" as Richard Péres-Peña has put it. But as you pursue the story, the facts of events, or "the surprise along the way," of which this research had a large share — especially as I pursued Mansureh's life story — tend to "blow it apart." As Péres-Peña puts it, "That is not what the reader usually sees. An article is, by definition, hindsight; it aims to make sense, in a condensed account, of what the reporter [historian, biographer, . . .] found, which can feel sprawling and confused while the reporting [the research] is underway." Is it possible for historians to write in a style that preserved "a feel for what it's like to be the reporter [the researcher] pursuing it"?[6]

For my project, a related issue was the question of how I positioned myself vis-à-vis the historical subjects in this manuscript. In a very fundamental way, tackling the problem of *how I positioned myself vis-à-vis the historical subjects in this manuscript* — a positioning that radically changed over the years of multiple rewritings — affected both my dealing with the ethical dilemmas, and how I was approaching my various sources, including family papers and pictures, the many informal conversations with relatives, family gossip, and rumors, as well as how I was using both the wwqi digital archive and historical documents in general.

Quite often, explicitly and more often implicitly through the narrative structure and arguments of the texts we write, we as historians position ourselves, to put it bluntly and simplistically, in the position of "I am smarter than my historical subjects, and I understand and can explain them, what they did, etc., better than themselves." Through many email conversations with Michael Amico, I felt even more strongly that our job as historians is to explain to our contemporary audience how our historical subjects saw the world, what they experienced at their time and place, and how to make sense of the choices they made. In other words, we attempt to tell our historical subjects' stories in a way that generates a sentiment of empathy, rather than judgment, in ourselves and in our audience.

For example, in some of the earlier versions of this book, how I told my mother's commitment to marriage for love was dominated by my own perplexity over how she, and other women and men since her generation, believed and continued to believe in marrying for love as a recipe for happiness, and as necessarily monogamous, despite what I had called, following Elizabeth A. Povinelli's observations, the unreferentiality of such expectations in facts. I wrote of this deep belief as an illusion, as what blinded and betrayed my mother. Not only did the notion of illusion run "the risk of getting us off on the wrong track, because it has an unpleasing suggestion of gullibility, simplistic and even offensive," the more difficult task turned out to be making that faith in, and desire for, marrying for love meaningful to myself and my readers, despite my own views on promises of a love marriage and monogamy.[7]

Similarly, at issue was not so much my disdain that modernists considered temporary marriage as prostitution, or arranged marriages as forced, but to bring to life how changes in conditions of life, including education of women and their pursuit of professional lives, and changes in the urban scene and structures of work and living spaces, generated the material conditions within which arranged marriage did come to be experienced as forced marriage, how the presumption of monogamy of companionate love marriage had come to emerge, and how temporary marriage became reconceived and projected as prostitution.

Approached thus, the meaning of various genres of documents and how we use them can change as well. Not only does gossip, for instance, remain an important source of knowledge, but its significance is no different from presumably more objective resources that can be fact-checked. As Arlette Farge has written in a different context, in neighborhoods where social life outside the home revolved around talk, where "making the smallest purchase requires endless verbiage, and lowering the price a few sous wears out the lungs of both parties, even extensive conversation in a room is not enough. It is customary to continue conversing in the doorway, on the landing, and all the way down the stairs."[8] Circulating words act as a source of social knowledge and critical life decisions. As Alain Corbin has written, within small communities, "when it became necessary to choose, or rather to procure, a spouse for this errant young lady, a whole squadron of informers was called into action: confessors and curés acted as marriage brokers; provincial relations acted as intelligence operatives; lawyers and notaries were employed to question their colleagues; bureaucrats were questioned about the virtues of their subordinates, and servants were sent out to gather rumors."[9]

Gossip and rumor work regardless of their truth status; they form in specific ways how people experience particular other facts of their lives. For instance, because there was rumor and gossip around my father's tendency to flirt with women, such gossip and rumor defined how my mother would experience his interactions with women at parties and other social occasions. It may have, as well, defined how other women flirted with my father.

To bring out the complexities of their time and place, the historical context and material conditions within which my parents lived, risks some of the pitfalls of historicism. As Amico has put it, "Historicism, in its call for an overarching set of characteristics of a time and place, has replaced them [here he is discussing specific relationships between people, "almost romantic friendship," "mutual, unselfish love and devotion to each other"] with ideas such as brotherhood and friendship. Individual relationships are then, in the fashion of Enlightenment thought, simply asserted as examples of an idea, a word to turn around and upside down, its boundaries still clear."[10] How does one contextualize without turning particular people into examples of general ideas, such as "modern woman," "enlightened man," and so on?

Amico's proposed style of contextualization, however, amounts to a different kind of reclaiming experience, not as some prediscursive ground for authority to speak (for the dead), but as an attempt to ground

> analysis in the subject's point of view "on the ground." The guideline I've used for myself is: A subject only acts (and actions include analyzing and narrating) within the constraints of the sources. This way I can better understand how ideas and thoughts and theories are generated by the historical subject, and myself. The material turns — whatever re-

ality brings—continue to disrupt the analyses and narratives along the way, producing moments of knotted blockages, like the one you find your mother experiencing. These then must be resolved by new ideas and narratives. So constraints are also opportunities. I wouldn't say that any one story or trope is non-referential, an empty idea, or delusional (three ideas you introduce in assessing your mother's understanding) but rather that these stories and tropes are themselves the attempt to surmount the obstacles of materiality, and that this process is what constitutes a traceable life. . . . This is related to thinking about basic dynamics of force and choice that can be felt by the reader as well, not as ideas but in terms of actual material developments and paths that facilitate, hide, or block people's way, and are then felt as impediments or new avenues of access in an individual's thought process or movement through space and time. . . . [H]ow contingent and inventive are the stories and histories and fantasies we tell to manage the truth of our desires. Is there any other way but to live through the forgetfulness of narrative . . . ? Narrative reveals and remembers and organizes and explains—yes, but *in order to do all that*, it also forgets. Forgetting, and trying to see past the blind spots and jump over the obstacles that confront us, seems to be inseparable at some level from generating a new life. I suppose the historian's job is to forget as transparently as possible. What the reader sees through the historian's way of telling a story are all the twists and turns along the way.[11]

At first, it seemed that shifting my position vis-à-vis my historical subjects magically made my ethical dilemma vanish: I would tell my parents' story from a position of deep empathy for both of them, explaining the choices they made within the material conditions of their time and place, including why they wanted the story not to be told and yet why I was telling it. That, clearly, would be a disingenuous claim to make. At the end, I made the decision of telling the story, despite such equivocations, and there is no way of escaping the ethical responsibility for that decision.

But perhaps as importantly, the effort to understand in its own time and place how people made the choices they did out of their given material reality required a different approach to reading my sources, hearing the family stories, gossip and rumors included, and seeing photographs and objects of daily life. Not only do deep interpretive readings, informed by hermeneutics of suspicion, and the search for hidden meanings become inappropriate, surface reading as well is inadequate, unless we reconceptualize the surface to cut across and connect many texts and documents of a given time and place, to read across many surfaces at once.

To do that kind of across-surface reading also requires using multiple genres of documents. People in the past, as we do today, did not just write letters, books, newspaper articles — all the usual textual material that composes the vast majority of archival sources used by most historians. These texts are intimately bound up with, and acquire their meaning from, the practices of everyday life. Even when we cannot witness these practices firsthand, we can find traces of them in objects, photographs, oral histories, and so on. By reading a text through related objects and spaces, in connection with sounds and memories, we can gain new insights that would be impossible to reach by reading the text alone. Working with family papers, photographs, kin accounts of past family events, and objects all make familial sleuthing easier and yet, at times, more risky — posing risks of overhearing mistakenly, over-reading harshly in hindsight.

And the question remains: How relevant is one family's story to a larger understanding of its time and place? Who, but I and my family, cares about my parents' marriage, secrets and all? If I resist making them "examples of ideas," what is the relevance of the story I tell? My hope is that things could work in the opposite direction: excavating my family history and contextualizing it through the stories of many other families' lives — some through interviews, some through the WWQI archive — in other words, by locating a few persons' stories within the world in which they lived and how they made their life story as they went along, can also open up ways of seeing the larger world around them. This approach brings closer together what presumably distinguishes the work of a historian from the work of a historical fiction writer. Amico's description of how he went about collecting his archive for his dissertation reads remarkably similar to how Amitav Ghosh explains his research for writing the Ibis trilogy — piecing together memoirs, newspapers, diaries, letters, other primary sources, and the many travels that would trace their characters. For Amico, those materials related to two actual Civil War participants; for Ghosh, his imagined characters. While a historical dissertation writer does not have some of the liberties that a historical fiction writer might have, at their best they have pulled very close to each other. I suspect many of us wish we could write our histories with the same richness of feeling of time and place that Ghosh succeeds in bringing out in his fiction.

I. Marrying for Love

My mother, Fari, had married my father, 'Abbas, when she was thirty years old—a rather late first marriage for her generation, perhaps even now. She had successfully warded off several familially arranged marriage proposals. She was determined, she had said again and again, to marry for love. A love marriage finally walked into her life when her sister's husband's nephew, 'Abbas, fell in love with her. He began to visit his uncle more often; he quit smoking after Fari had once opened a window with disdain to let the smoke out. He soon asked for her hand. Fari and 'Abbas were married on 14 January 1942.

Fari's resistance against a familially arranged marriage and the desire for a marriage of her choosing, based on knowing and socializing with her future husband, a desire for a marriage of mutual affection and love, was not unique to her. By the 1930s, modern education and professional careers had enabled many urban middle-class women to think of marriage as something to do with their individual lives, as a choice made by a woman and a man, rather than as a family affair (an alliance based on negotiation between two families). Educational and professional spaces also provided the opportunity for kin-unrelated women and men to meet, know each other, and make decisions about their future spouse.

This by no means implies that marriages in Iran, even today, are no longer "family affairs." The embeddedness of individuals in family life continues to inform marriage decisions and practices. The two families being of a similar sociocultural status (*kufu*) weighs on all marriage choices. In practice, even couples who meet at work or educational establishments, and socialize for a sustained period of time before making a marriage decision, go through the same practices: sending the man's family to the woman's family to ask for her hand, and so on.

The emerging expectation about marrying someone whom you got to know and love prior to marriage also generated a different expectation about the process through which marriage came about. While the ritual of a man's family visiting the potential bride's family to ask for her hand continued (and continues in many marriages up to now), women came to expect their knowledge and approval as a necessary step; they expected to have a say in the selection of their future husband. Resisting and warding off unwanted suitors became part of the game. This changing expectation also contributed to arranged marriages without the woman's participation being experienced as a forced parental imposition.

In her interviews and memoirs, conducted and written in the late 1980s and early 1990s, Fari took great pleasure in telling the story of warding off people who came to ask for her hand in marriage (*khvastgari*): "When someone came to our house for khvastgari, we [she and her sisters] made trouble; we made rude gestures. I remember once we made faces and they never came back. Gradually fewer people would come."[1] Among her *khvastgars* were several on Fari's mother's side of the family. They were observant of the hijab and the related gender-separation rules. There was no way, Fari said, she would marry into those families. As a young, educated, working woman, she would have had to give up much that mattered to her.

Similar warding-off stories are recorded in memoirs of other women of that generation. It is a recurrent theme in Giti Afruz's diaries. "Mihrpur came over with two women I didn't know. First, I thought they were my mother's acquaintances; then I realized they had something in mind [eyeing her for their son or a male relative].... I burst into laughter uncontrollably,... eventually I made a thousand faces and gestures, which repelled them."[2]

Simin Bihbihani narrates her mother's recollections about how Simin had repeatedly warded off khvastgars. In one case, when, as was the custom, she had taken in a tray of tea and offered it to the visiting lady, the woman had given her an appraising look "from head to toe, taken the tea, and turning to your father said, 'hijab is a woman's adornment.' You retorted: 'under the hijab one can be more deceitful.' Then you put down the tray and left the room.... [Y]our father didn't talk to you for a month."[3]

These changing ideas, about what constitutes, or ideally ought to constitute, the family, and linked with it the meaning of marriage, were not unique to Iran. New ideas about personal, family, and societal life spread across a region that is now divided into many nation-states but that had been, until the late nineteenth and early twentieth centuries, part of the Ottoman domain and Qajar Iran. Initially affecting a small segment of the urban cultural elite of social and political reformers, these ideas began to spread to a growing layer of the population, especially in large urban centers, over a relatively short time. As many scholars have shown, two critical entwined changes occurred. First, the ideal of family shifted from a generationally expansive and at times polygynous structure to become a *conjugally centered* (rather than seniority-focused) family. My mother, living her married life with her husband's mother, had complained about her generationally expansive arrangement because her mother-in-law's presence disrupted the conjugality of her home.

Second, the ideal marriage became a *companionate* and preferably monogamous marriage chosen by the partners, rather than arranged by families, and based on deep affection (*muhibbat*), if not love (*'ishq*). Even if love did not precede marriage, the conjugally centered marriage was expected to generate affection between the couple as they lived and shared life together.[4]

These ideas were, from the start, intimately linked with notions of the nation, patriotic aspirations, what constituted the modern, and the changing structure of governance that was to shift from elite household-integrated patterns of personalized and family patronage toward centralized, civil bureaucracies operating on an ideal of impersonal management of government. But how do we understand the hold of these ideas not simply on the political and intellectual elite discourses, but on the imagination of the growing urban middle class, in particular among a growing layer of urban women? How did the ideas of the companionate (monogamous) marriage and the conjugal couple as family gain their near imperial hegemony, to borrow Elizabeth A. Povinelli's term?[5]

Povinelli works with the idea of the near-imperial hegemony of love in the context of liberal settler colonies (and progressive queers in the United States) in comparison to a small community of men and women in the Northern Territory of Australia, over the course of the late nineteenth century into the twentieth.[6] She analyzes "how discourses of individual freedom and social constraint — what [she refers] to as *autological* and *genealogical* imaginaries — animate and enflesh love, sociality, and bodies; how they operate as strategic maneuvers of power whose purpose — or result — is to distribute life, goods, and values across social spaces; and how they contribute to the hardiness of liberalism as a normative horizon."[7] Povinelli further claims that "the intimate couple is a key transfer point between, on the one hand, liberal imaginaries of contractual economies, politics, and sociality and, on the other, liberal forms of power in the contemporary world. Love, as an intimate event, secures the self-evident goodness of social institutions, social distributions of life and death, and social responsibilities for these institutions and distributions."[8] She pursues the question of "the intimate event," as "related to the sovereign subject, and how it secures its legitimacy vis-à-vis the negative image of the genealogical society."[9] It is in this context that she asks: "How, then, do these discourses deepen their grip on social life though they are internally unstable and referentially untrue? The maintenance of intimate sovereignty as a truth of liberal empire depends on a method of constituting three kinds of truth about the subjects and objects of empire: the truth of intimacy's proper domain, the truth of its normative ideals, and the truth of contrasting evils that surround it."[10]

My line of argument here is inspired by Povinelli's arguments, with a difference: I am looking at the fractures and lines of differentiation *within* Iranian society, which had begun to take shape since at least the mid-nineteenth century, between a modernist desire for an imagined future *autological* society and its demarcation from a present/past imaginary of the *genealogical* society that was constricting the choices aspired for by the modernists. In that context as well, "the intimate couple is a key transfer point." In the context of early twentieth-century Iran, the power of the concept of love-based marriage (and perceived as monogamous by women) and of a conjugally centered household — the truth of its normative ideal — depended (and continues to depend) on the co-emergent self-evident evilness of arranged marriage and polygyny, and the desire for a preferably not-generationally expansive household.[11] In Ottoman domains, polygyny was often configured in relation to slavery and concubinage.[12] In Iran part of the foil against which monogamy developed its ideational power was mutʿa (sigheh) marriages — fixed-time marriages for sexual pleasure, often considered in modernist discourse to be a veneer for prostitution. The love-based companionate marriage was to be monogamous *and* to last for life.

As scholars writing about similar developments in Ottoman Turkey and Egypt have noted, polygyny was statistically insignificant (though the possibility of it hung over one's marriage). A 2003 report on Iran indicated that the percentage of men with more than one wife has continued to decline from 3.1 percent in 1976 to 1.2 percent in 1986 to 0.08 percent in 1995.[13] Additionally, there is no evidence-based study to demonstrate that arranged marriages were necessarily or largely experienced as forced (even when resented, it could possibly be experienced or at least expressed as fate — *qismat*), nor that most households were indeed multigenerational over much of one's life cycle. Mari Ladieh-Fuladi's report in 2003 indicates that a local study in Shiraz indicated that 1,049 out of 1,242 families in the study were "nuclear" and only 193 families had "more complex" structures.[14] Following Povinelli, I suggest that the emerging and sustained notion of polygyny and arranged marriage as evidently evil has intimately depended on the life of the co-emergent idea of the self-evident goodness of the monogamous, companionate marriage. The lives of these ideas have mutually regenerated and sustained each other. Who could be against love and freedom of choice? Who could advocate arranged marriage (now experienced, at least by educated urban women, as forced familial imposition)? Who could possibly be happy to share her husband with another wife?

Moreover, on an ideational level, a connection between dreaded venereal diseases and male promiscuity seems to have become part of the self-evident superiority of monogamy by the 1930s and 1940s.[15] A key perceived effect of the spread of such diseases was seen to be infertility of the wives. This became another foil against which monogamy drew its ideational power. Family examples of infertility of wives caused by their husbands' venereal diseases, in particular gonorrhea, became powerfully worked into the undesirability of polygyny — against not only taking more than one permanent wife, but also having sigheh marriages.

Among my father's side of the family, three such stories circulated. First, there was A'miz Mammad Khan, an uncle of my grandmother (Nuri Khanum), who was an officer in Riza Shah's army — a key bastion where soldiers and officers were said to get and spread venereal diseases. Indeed, the opposition to compulsory conscription in the 1930s and 1940s was in part articulated through how the army would corrupt the young men's virtues and make them vulnerable to contracting such diseases. A'miz Mammad Khan and his wife never had children, and the family rumor was that he had passed his disease to her.

Next, there was Nuri Khanum's sister, Sadiqeh Khanum. She married her first husband, Dr. Ahmad Khan, in December 1924. They had one child, a son who died before reaching the age of two; their marriage ended in divorce in March 1933. Sadiqeh Khanum was said to have become infertile, as a consequence of Ahmad Khan's venereal disease.[16] Married a second time to Ziya' Najmabadi (on 25 April 1944), Sadiqeh Khanum never conceived another child. Lastly, my father's uncle 'Isa, who had married my mother's sister 'Iffat, was said to have rendered 'Iffat infertile.

While inspired by Povinelli's propositions, I do want to note an important qualification. Her propositions work well regarding the *broad* level of societal changes and teleological observations, looking at actors in the past from where the historian or theorist writes today. What works for the level of the *individual's* desire for a companionate marriage, or the hope of something better, in their specific time, is examining what they saw around them, how they processed their own experiences and the experiences of others in their life. That is what historians need to do: to explain people's past experiences to today's readers, rather than presume that we can understand people in the past, and their choices and practices, better than they did.

To return to my mother's example, Fari's decision to marry for love was not simply living an emerging dominating idea, obtained from reading novels and watching silent movies of the 1930s. She witnessed varying practices of marriage all around her. In later years, she recounted many of those marriages as failures (including two of her older sisters), but others in more positive terms. In her narrative, every instance was directly linked to whether the marriage had been arranged by the elders or entered into by partners who had come to know and like each other before getting married. Fari's eldest sister's marriage, for example, had been arranged by the two families. Her husband, in the family's semihushed lore, was more inclined to young male adolescents than to women. Her sister spent many years in a terribly unhappy marriage, before she finally obtained a divorce. Unlike Fari's younger sisters, she had not continued school after her graduation from middle school. As importantly, in Fari's narrative, she had never held a job. Her husband's father had been a very rich money changer (*sarraf*) and they had lived off his wealth.

Fari's third sister's marriage had been arranged through a friend recommending her to the groom's family. That too ended in divorce. The one important difference, in Fari's narrative, was that this sister had continued her education and was a working woman. Indeed, Fari emphasized that the importance of education for girls ("I was grateful that my father was enlightened and sent us all to school") was that it permitted them to work and thus leave bad marriages.

Fari had witnessed terrible marriages for these two sisters, but she also had the example of another older sister, 'Iffat, who, like her, resisted arranged marriage. Only at the age of thirty-six did 'Iffat finally meet someone at work whom she liked and eventually married. Being working women, with their own income and a career, offered alternative visions of a desired life for 'Iffat and Fari, including a desired marriage.

The argument that the power of the concepts of love-based, monogamous marriage and of a conjugally centered household depends on the co-emergent self-evident evilness of arranged marriage, of polygyny, of sigheh/mut'a (in Iran's case), and of generationally expansive families risks its reversal: does this indicate a nostalgia for arranged marriage and polygyny, to put it most bluntly?[17] This powerful reversal contributes to constituting the self-evident goodness of the first set of ideas—as if always we have no other way out of the historically co-emergent terms. To borrow from Svetlana Boym's discussion of nostalgia as taboo, invoking nostalgia as a warning is meant to protect us against a fearful fate: "the predicament of Lot's wife, a fear that looking back might paralyze you forever, turning you into a pillar of salt, a pitiful monument to your own grief."[18]

Even more critically, historians are at times worried about how nostalgia interferes with their work. Heghnar Watenpaugh, for instance, has argued that nostalgia can "displace the crafting of history, or historical investigation. In this sense, nostalgia interferes with and prevents a critical recollective approach to the past. It preempts and prevents a critical engagement with the past, among other things, and encourages a regressive retreat into comforting memories of an imaginary past."[19] But introducing a delineation between nostalgia and history is itself a particular approach to doing history, which sees the task of the historian as recovering and explaining "what actually happened," *without* taking into account what could have happened but did not, and how the meaning of what did happen in part depends on other possibilities *not* happening. Considering nostalgia "as a mode of memory" would bring it back into the process of crafting history, rather than being an impediment to it. Again, to quote Boym, the nostalgia considered in this sense is not "for the ancién regime . . . but . . . for the unrealized dreams of the past and vision of the future that became obsolete . . . for unrealized possibilities, unpredictable turns and crossroads."[20] She proposes incorporation of nostalgia in what she calls an *off-modern* fashion, to make "us explore sideshows and back alleys rather than the straight road of progress; it allows us to take a detour from the deterministic narrative of twentieth-century history."[21]

Bringing nostalgia back into historical imagination may help us imagine affinities that existed, could have continued to exist, but no longer exist. It may help convey a sense of sentiments and affects associated with particular memories of events, at times through visual effects of photographs, of feelings of space in the case of residential buildings and changing neighborhoods. It may also help us appreciate the living, complex familial practices, despite the dominance of the ideal family as conjugally centered.

Romantic Novels and Moral Tales

The entry of love as an appropriate sentiment to inform marriage in Iran goes back to the later decades of the nineteenth century. Transformation of the concept of love was a key marker of Iranian modernity: heteronormalization of sexual mores and heterosocialization of public life called for re-envisioning marriage from a procreative, family-centered contract to a love-based, conjugally focused concept. As I have argued more fully elsewhere, modernist intellectuals began to condemn arranged and sigheh marriages, advocating marriage based on affection, love, and choice.[22] Initially, this turned out to be a hard sell. When a later generation of intellectuals turned to issues of love, sexuality, and marriage at the turn of the twentieth century, two genres, both with a tragic narrative logic, were most popular. First, there were the romantic tales, dynamized by national reform imperatives. In these novels, the possibility of a happy ending was frustrated by such obstacles as existing concepts of marriage, parental control over the choice of spouse, differential expectations by men and women, lack of modern education for women, unconscionability of men of religion and state, all the way to the autocracy of governments. Such tragic closures contained the possibility of happiness: removal of autocracy, educational and legal reforms, and cultural transformations concerning gender and sexuality would make it possible to rewrite the story with a happy ending.

The political work of such novels, often first serialized in newspapers, was recognized by reformers. Shaykh Ibrahim Zanjani, a young cleric advocate of constitutional ideas, who later served as a member of the first four sessions of the Iranian parliament (Majlis), recalls in his memoirs that from his hometown of Zanjan, in the years before the Constitutional Revolution, he would ask his friends in Tehran to send him, in addition to writings of Talibuf, and books such as *Siyahatnamah-i Ibrahim Bayg,* "new novels [*roman*] to help awaken people against autocracy, oppression, and warning against superstitious and deceptive ideas of pseudo-scholars of Islam."[23]

This early association between two modernist aspirations—reform of the political system and reform of the patriarchal family—worked to produce the self-evident goodness of the latter once the self-evident goodness of the former became a political consensus, at least among large sections of the urban middle class. "Who could be against a parliamentary system in place of the old autocratic government?" cast its supportive cloak over "who could be against a choice marriage in place of a familially arranged one?" Familially mediated and arranged marriages were associated tightly with the autocratic governmental workings of the Qajars—a system, since its formation in the early nineteenth century, based on the appointment of variously kin-connected aristocrats or local tribal chiefs, whose daughters were married to the king and to other men of power. Indeed, the latter's power drew on such kin associations, a governmental system based on traffic in women. It was this style of governance that the Constitutionalists aspired to replace with a system built around the Majlis, modern government offices, and books of regulations, replacing autocratic arbitrariness with bureaucratic predictability. In a parallel fashion, the family-mediated and arranged marriages would be replaced by young men and women meeting each other prior to marriage, developing bonds of affection, and deciding their own marriage choices (*intikhab*, meaning "choice," but in this period also becoming the word to refer to the election of parliamentarians). The parents, in this thinking, were expected to at least seek their children's, in particular their daughters,' *ra'y* (here meaning "opinion" but also in this period coming to mean parliamentary vote) before making such an arrangement. Intikhab and ra'y became desirable both in politics and in personal life.

The second, and somewhat later, genre of early twentieth-century novels were the moral tales of warning about urban corruption and abusive men who took advantage of naïve, young (often rural, immigrant) women in the new climate of urban gender heterosocialization.[24] Here too moral corruption and abuse were tightly mapped to governmental corruption and abuse. The male abusers were often aristocrats and/or top government functionaries. Possibly the best-known example of this genre was Muhammad Hijazi's *Ziba*, first published in 1930. As M. Ghanoonparvar has noted, "Critics generally regard *Zibā*, Ḥejāzi's third novel, as his best work, mainly because it contains, along with his usual didactic moral messages of virtue and chastity, a most detailed and frank fictional record of governmental, political, and bureaucratic corruption, a subject matter which has been of great interest to the mainstream, socially conscious writers in Persia for more than a century." After a thorough summary and discussion of the novel, Ghanoonparvar rightly concludes, "By and large, *Zibā* is a novel of disillusionment. While Ḥosayn finally realizes that absolute power is only a mirage and that his efforts to gain it have only resulted in the destruction of himself and his family, Zibā's dream to have a family some day is also no more than an illusion in a society that uses and shuns her."[25]

The disciplinary effects of these tales on a generation of women about to participate in the emerging heterosocializing culture of modern urbanity can be imagined. For young women, the desire for love-based marriage, and resistance against marriage arranged by families, would be controlled by fear of the consequences of such desire as emplotted in these tragic tales of deceit. Such consequences were often suicide, death from venereal diseases, or, at (illegitimate) childbirth.

How did the idea of love-based marriage travel from the political modernist discourse of small circles of intellectuals and reform newspapers to become what a growing number of (initially) urban middle-class, young people, in particular women, expected of their marriages?

Early in the century, marrying for love was still reported as if in the category of "strange and wondrous things" (*'ajayib*). One newspaper, *Nauruz*, in its 16 August 1903 issue, under the heading "Love" on page 7 reported, as worthy of note, the formation of a society by American girls who had vowed not to marry except through love — they would either fall in love or be loved. Within a couple of decades, marrying for love was circulating as an idea pertinent to domestic lives in Iran.

The work of reform newspapers as a medium for circulation of ideas went beyond small circles. The idea of marrying for love was possibly generated in part by what young people were reading in the early decades of the twentieth century, in newspapers and increasingly in books of fiction. This is surely what critics, such as Ahmad Kasravi, clamored against: reading novels was corrupting the youth. As Amy Motlagh has argued, Kasravi "criticized the genre [the novel] as a dangerous import from the West that blurred the boundaries between the real and the unreal."[26]

The new reading habits were also held responsible and criticized for such dissemination within the works of fiction themselves. In Murtiza Mushfiq Kazimi's *Tihran-i makhauf*, the father of Mahin, the central female character, hears that his daughter is in love with her cousin Farrukh; he considers this love as a serious impediment to his plans for marrying her to the son of an aristocrat through whose influence he hopes to become elected to the Majlis. When he finds out that she has been reading books that speak of love, that is, novels, he notes, "Now I understand why this ignorant girl speaks of such things. . . . [S]he has been reading that so-and-so fell in love with so-and-so, and has thus concluded that she too is in love with her cousin. . . . In our days, we read books like *Amir Arsalan*, *Iskandarnameh*, and *Husayn Kurd*, and we had no shortcomings not speaking of love and falling in love. What was wrong with that? Now, we have to hear all this, all the fault of the new schools. What is wrong with me who has never read a single novel?"[27]

Within the emerging world of early Iranian fiction, tradition-minded parents were often depicted as holding the modern educational establishments responsible for putting the wrong ideas into young people's heads. In *Ruzgar-i siyah* (Dark days; 1924) — the story of a prostitute, 'Iffat, and several of her friends and co-workers — 'Iffat is from a rich, upper-middle-class family, with an old-fashioned mother who was against modern education and schooling for girls and who later blames the schools for her daughter's resistance against the marriage her parents have had to arrange to cover up her missteps that had brought shame to the family: "Damn that school that taught you to be so rude and demanding. Do you think here is Europe where you can choose a husband of your own liking?"[28]

Similarly, in *Tihran-i makhauf*, it is this very education that is depicted as what makes Mahin to speak of love, fall in love, and have her own idea of whom she wants to marry. It enables her to stand her ground, speak back to her parents, resist her parents' choice, and insist on her own path. Writing to her mother, after eloping with her cousin Farrukh to escape the marriage arranged against her will by her parents, she elaborates:

I had explicitly expressed my unwillingness to accept as my husband the person that you and my father had chosen according to your wishes, and disregarding what I wanted. . . . Alas, you were not prepared to consider my opinion and desire [ra'y and *mayl*] concerning my future spouse, but instead you insisted on trying to make me enchained to a man for whom I feel not the slightest affection in my heart. Perhaps if I were a thoughtless girl, and did not take the important matter of marriage seriously, I would have accepted the hand of the first person asking for my hand. . . . But unfortunately, or fortunately, I do not see the important matter of marriage only through the 'aqd [marriage contract] and 'arusi [marriage celebration] ceremonies. . . . I see these as the beginning of a new period, perhaps a long period, of living a happy life in the company of a husband chosen by my heart. . . . If you want to participate in the happy life of Farrukh and I sooner than later, please try to persuade my father to give his consent to our marriage; . . . otherwise, we may not meet again in the near future. . . . . Forget that Farrukh is my cousin, or that he does not have much wealth; remember his deeds and good manners, and know that he is my beloved, my soul, my life, and finally my future husband.[29]

The pitting of individual choice (depicted in these novels as moved by love) against parental imposition (often driven by a father's greed and lust for power, and/or by a mother's ignorance, illiteracy, and subservience to her husband) contributed to the generation of familially arranged marriage, often depicted (and experienced by women) as forced (*ijbari*), as being one of the foils against which love-based marriage acquired its self-evident goodness.

Yet, despite critics such as Kasravi who blamed the novel for the youth's misguided ideas, or even as articulated through the parental outrage within novels such as *Ruzgar-i siyah* and *Tihran-i makhauf*, holding women's education responsible for enabling them to read fiction and become misguidedly desirous of love, love as depicted in numerous novels of this period was paradoxically rarely a good thing!

In most of Hijazi's didactic fiction, including *Parichihr* (first published in 1929), *Ziba*, *Parvaneh*, and *Sirishk*, love is a destructive passion, not a sentiment out of which family life could be shaped. On the contrary, it is a force that destroys the family. Hijazi's criticism, in novel after novel, and the popularity of his novels seem to speak more to a panic over popular circulation of love as such. Yet these novels at the same time reinforced the idea that love is good but only if it is contained within the formation of family, as is the case in *Huma* (first published in 1927).[30] As Ghanoonparvar notes, "*Homā* is an idealistic representation of a modern Persian woman, or at least what Ḥejāzi and many of his readers would have liked to believe and obviously, as his later works indicate, perhaps a model to be emulated by other women."[31] Even in this novel, Huma's eventual marriage is not to the man with whom she was in love (and he with her). But here it is Huma who steps back from agreeing to marry him because she learns that he already has a wife and children in Isfahan. At this point in the novel, Huma goes on to give a long discourse on how men are cruel to women, and that she would never marry a married man and make another woman miserable. As a result, eventually, the man does the right thing and returns to his family.

As one of the exceptional happy-ending tales of this genre, *Huma* is a narrative lesson (*dastan-i 'ibrat*) on the advantages of solid education, responsible love, and wisdom. As Claus Pedersen concludes, "'Homa' is first and foremost a love story, where morals and a balanced relation between emotions and reason lie at the heart of the novel."[32] It also provides a criticism of bigamy through a woman's voice.

Of course, readers always engage in partial readings; one could love being in love, including fiery, lustful love, and, contrary to authorial intentions, attribute the terrible things that ensue to other causes than "fire on the soul," as Hijazi called love. But in any case, it is difficult to propose that these novels were advocating love-based marriage as such. After all, in *Tihran-i makhauf*, Mahin's pursuit of a love-based marriage ends in her death—though clearly the villains were her parents, not love. Subsequently, in the second volume, *Yadigar-i yik shab* (Memento of the one night), familial contentment is finally attained, between Farrukh and a former prostitute, 'Iffat, whom he had rescued from a brothel in the previous volume.[33] The sentiment that 'Iffat feels for Farrukh, which will slowly be reciprocated, unlike the sentiment between Farrukh and Mahin, is never named love, or 'ishq. She is at first deeply grateful but is gripped with an emotional upheaval (*inqilab-i halat*). In her heart, she "senses a strange feeling towards Farrukh, but could Farrukh possibly consider her anything but a sister?"[34] By the end of the second volume, Farrukh and 'Iffat do get married, yet any feeling between them, including what Farrukh eventually begins to develop for 'Iffat, is never named "love." Instead, other words of affection, such as *'alaqeh*, *muhibbat*, and *dust dashtan*, are used to name "this strange feeling." To name it "love," the target of this sentiment needed to be an educated woman, such as Mahin, not a former prostitute.

In this literary production, the sentiment named "love" between a modern, educated, young man and woman, such as Farrukh and Mahin, is indeed a new love, and different from the despised homoerotic love of classical Persian literature that Kasravi, among others, attacked. Being an effect of modern education and new reading habits, it is also not yet accessible to the lower classes and uneducated folk. 'Iffat—a girl born into a privileged urban family but who did not pursue an education and was married off seemingly well by her parents to a man who prostituted her—as we saw, did not have the language for naming the "strange feeling" she had developed toward her rescuer Farrukh. When in the second volume affection develops between a lower-class man and woman, Javad and Jalalat, the innocent girl, Jalalat, "did not know what to name this strange feeling."[35] Jalalat's problem is shared by Javad: "Their knowledge did not permit their describing their hearts' feelings for each other appropriately; they had not read anything but books such as *Chihil tuti* and *Iskandarnameh*."[36] While the author does name the sentiment between the two as love ('ishq) by calling them (once) lover (*'ashiq*) and beloved (*ma'shuq*), the characters themselves do not know how to name this feeling.[37]

With the exception of *Huma*, there is not any explicit link between even an affection-based marriage and monogamy. Indeed, monogamy and its ob-

verse, polygyny, are virtually absent from these novels, even though as Pedersen has noted, "There is no doubt about the fact that the common denomina-
tor of the social realist novels... is the theme 'women' and their conditions in
early 20th century Iran. There is also agreement in the three novels [*Tihran-i
makhauf*, *Ruzgar-i siyah*, and *Huma*] that the causes of women's sad conditions are traditions like compulsory marriage and child marriage, the lack of
education for girls and the general low status of women in society."[38]

Satire

Fiction was not the exclusive domain for articulation of the themes of the
terrible conditions of women and of compulsory and child marriage. Nor
were these themes newly explored in the 1920s and 1930s. After all, much late
nineteenth-century sociopolitical criticism, written as fiction among other
genres, had already started a line of association between the political and cultural backwardness of the country and women's conditions.

There are, however, two significant differences. By the early decades of
the twentieth century, there was a larger and growing reading public, including women. Moreover, these novels were short, often first serialized in newspapers and then printed in relatively cheap editions. They were thus more
accessible and circulated among a larger population.

From the mid-nineteenth century onward, a new genre of writing and
performance, satirical plays, was among the first places in which issues of
marriage, including strong criticism of polygyny, were discussed. Best known
among these playwriters was the essayist Mirza Fath'ali Akhundzadeh. As
Sheida Dayani has articulated, "The idea of 'moral refinement' for 'the nation of Islam' with the common tropes of polygamy, arranged marriage, temporary marriage, women's rights, gender equality, education, rationality,
legal corruption, and the rule of law appear both in the plays and in the non-
dramatic writings of Akhundzadeh."[39]

Most importantly, the impact of Akhundzadeh's plays, read by literate intellectuals and other reformers, should be considered, because the audience
for these plays was far wider than for his political epistles. As Dayani demonstrates, Akhundzadeh's choice of a theatrical play was thought through in
terms of the audience he wanted to reach for his criticism of issues to do
with women's position; he could not reach this audience with his political
tracts. Dayani quotes Akhundzadeh, as he concluded one of his letters, that
"because his comedy is written with critique and ridicule, it is far more effec-

tive in changing human behavior than the book of fatherly advice."[40] Dayani analyzes at length his two most popular plays, *The Defense Lawyers* and *The Vizier of Lankaran's Governor*.[41] In both plays, Akhundzadeh's criticism is sharply focused on arranged marriage, polygamy, and sigheh marriages.

In addition to satirical plays, political journalism began to criticize polygynous practices. At times, satirical press, going back to *Mulla Nasr al-Din*, wrote about the miserable lives of men with more than one wife, and the terrible lot of a wife facing her husband's new marriage, usually to a much younger woman. A political and sociocultural satirical weekly in Turkish published from 1906 to 1931, in Tiblisi, Tabriz, and Baku, *Mulla Nasr al-Din* has become particularly associated with criticism of old family and marital practices, including marrying off very young girls, polygyny, mut'a marriages, triple divorces, and sexual relations between adult men and adolescent males. *Mulla Nasr al-Din* had a large readership in Iran. In its fifth issue (5 May 1906) on page 2 it reported that its previous issue had been published in 25,000 copies, and more than half of the customers were from Khurasan, Tehran, Isfahan, Tabriz, and some rural areas. In the pages of *Mulla Nasr al-Din*, criticism of familial relations was an indication of Islamic-Iranian sociocultural backwardness, compared to European norms of family.[42]

In the early decades of the twentieth century, we also have sustained criticism of men's prerogatives in marriage, including polygyny and easy divorce, in the pages of the women's press and women's writings in reform newspapers. Here and in later women's advocacies of the 1920s and 1930s, such criticism is invoked to argue for women's education and reform of family law.

Yet rarely, either in the satirical plays of Akhundzadeh, in the political journalism of *Mulla Nasr al-Din*, or in the pages of the women's press, were the criticisms of polygyny and arranged marriage explicitly linked with advocacy of love-based marriage. One possible exception is perhaps

> Mirza Aqa Tabrizi's *Aqa Hashem-e Khalkhali*. . . . [T]his too is an advocacy of marrying for love as opposed to arranged marriage, but in essence, it is advocating monogamous marriages. Although the mention is brief, a polygamous marriage is associated with the stock character of the villain (warlock/fortune-teller), who claims that he was able to deflect the love of a man from his most desired wife (*sogoli*). I read that as the polygamous marriage being in the same or as much trouble as arranged marriage, thus both seeking witchcraft. In addition to warning against mut'a, the play also attributes honor-killing to the classic

villain, the girl's father (and her brothers). Add to that the criticism of the father having the only say and the mother not knowing any better and admitting to being *nāqes al-ʿaql*. Notably, Akhundzadeh criticized the heroine's independence in this play and told Tabrizi to rewrite her character.[43]

Farang

Oral circulation of what marital relations of Europeans (known as *farang* in Iran) were like may have also informed Iranian men's and women's ideas of a desirable match and a good marriage. Writing in her 1894 manuscript of *Maʿayib al-rijal* (Vices of men), Bibi Khanum Astarabadi criticized the possibly European-educated writer of a misogynous text, *Disciplining Women*, who advised men to treat their wives with severity and women to obey their husbands.[44] The author, she writes, is ignorant of the fact that all Europeans (*tamam-i ahl-i farang*) practice what is also recommended in classical wisdom in Arabic and Persian; they treat women like flowers, respect and serve them, and are in relations of unison and cordiality (*ittihad va ittifaq*) with them.[45]

As Amy Stanley has argued, albeit in a different context, the hearing and overhearing of stories were aspiration generating: in Bibi Khanum's case, a desire for better treatment of women; in the memoirs of Taj al-Saltaneh, a desire to go to Europe; or for my mother Fari's generation of urban, educated women, a desire for a love-based, conjugally focused marriage.[46]

Beyond "overhearing," as Bibi Khanum indicates about how "all Europeans" treated their women, women's memoirs (recollected and written decades later) indicate that the circulation of these ideas through new reading practices was informative of their marriage aspirations, if not always practices.

Mihrmah Farmanfarmayan (1915–2013) grew up in the large Farman-farma household in Tehran in the early decades of the twentieth century. Like many girls from Tehrani urban, upper-class families, she attended the Tarbiyat School for Girls and Zhandark and learned French for a foreign language.[47] Speaking of marriage, in a conversation with her older sister Maryam (Maryam Firuz, 1913–2008) and their gardener's daughter Maʿsumeh about to be married off, she writes, "We didn't have contact with the outside world, but used to read French novels in which always two young people wanted/desired each other [*khvahan-i yikdigar mi-shudand*] and married each other."[48] Yet, imagining her own future fate, she writes, "The expectation of us girls who grew up in the inner quarters [*andaruni*] and in houses far from the men's world was . . . formed by the certainty that beyond the high walls of the andaruni, . . . there were attractive highly educated men who would want/ desire us, . . . and who would one day come . . . and ask for our hand in marriage."[49] The trust in paternal judgment was definitely strong in the Farmanfarma household. Married in 1935, before departing from her father, Mihrmah asked him to write in her journal. He wished her happiness with her husband, ending with the advice to "always, as far as possible, obey your husband."[50]

The tension between the idea of desiring someone and getting married to that person, as Mihrmah had read in French novels, and how she had been married and advised by her father runs through many of the stories of this generation of women. For more middling urban women, such as my mother, her sisters, and work colleagues, their education provided a different mediation with the world outside the walls of their houses.

Bihbihani's mother's experience, as narrated by her daughter, exemplifies as well this different mediation, education and pursuit of a career, for meeting one's future spouse. Fakhr 'Uzma Arghun (1898–1966) was educated at home as well as at Zhandark and the American School. She wrote poetry and is described as an avid reader of newspapers, among them *Iqdam*, edited by 'Abbas Khalili. Reading his writings, she had imagined herself in love with him. She had sent him one of her patriotic poems for publication, which he promptly printed in *Iqdam*. He in turn had developed a fascination with this educated, young woman; he arranged for an occasion to visit her father, and subsequently he sent his mother and sister to ask for her hand. Their marriage started as if an enactment of a modern love-marriage script between a modern, young man and an educated, modern woman, though she was immediately gripped by doubts. On their wedding night, she wondered whom she had been in love with: The newspaper *Iqdam*? Khalili's essays? His novels? Or a man whom she had not seen very well yet, nor knew much about his temperament?[51]

For some of the men of this generation, education in Europe had reportedly provided familiarity with European family norms. 'Abd al-Husayn Mu'azzaz al-Mulk (Taymurtash), born in 1884, had been sent by his father first to Ashkhabad at the age of thirteen, then to the Saint Petersburg military academy. Upon returning to Iran at the age of twenty-four, he began working as a translator at the Ministry of Foreign Affairs in Tehran, and joined the Constitutionalists. Not much is known about his life over the next year or so, until the end of Muhammad ʿAli Shah's reign in July 1909. On 9 April 1909, Taymurtash was contractually married (ʿaqd) to Surur al-Saltaneh. In all likelihood, it was a familially arranged marriage.[52] Surur al-Saltaneh and Taymurtash did not live together immediately—not an uncommon process. Their wedding festivities had to wait for over a year. In the meantime, Taymurtash visited his bride occasionally and wrote letters in between visits.[53]

Two things are worth noting in these letters. First, the language in them is very different from some of the other spousal, affectionate letters we have from the Qajar period. And it is not only different from that of the early nineteenth-century minister and litterateur, Qaʾim Maqam, as one would expect, but also different from the language in the letters of the more traditionally educated Mirza Hasan Shaykh al-Islam to his three wives, all belonging roughly to the same period as those of Taymurtash. Qaʾim Maqam's and Mirza Hasan Shaykh al-Islam's letters indicate deep affectionate bonds between husband and wife.[54] Taymurtash's language is that of a passionate love, somewhat of a synthesis between the language of old Persian love poetry and that of European romantic fiction. It shares this language with other European-educated men of the period, such as Nusrat al-Saltaneh, some two decades later, writing from Europe to his wife, Aʿzam al-Saltaneh—these men were all educated in classical Persian literature and were readers (and sometimes translators) of contemporary European fiction.

Second, Taymurtash articulates his vision of what he desires for their marital bond, drawing a contrast between what he observes around him in Tehran of 1909–1910 and what he knows of farang. In one letter, he writes:

> I have told you a couple of times: in Iran, they don't understand love/ʿishq and affection/muhibbat. . . . [M]ost Iranian men seek pleasure [ʿaysh] and love-making [muʿashiqeh] outside their own homes. Instead of being in love with their own wives, instead of love-making with their own wives and not seeking foreign maîtresses, they forgo [the love of] their own wives. But in Farang, this is less of a problem and its shamefulness [viqahat] is much more than in Iran. Because usually man and woman love each other and prefer each other over all others. On the other hand, it is difficult to count this as a shortcoming of Iranians; often, the poor folk, from the age of five or six, without any volition and desire [ikhtiyar and mayl], have become bride and groom and there is no personal choice [raʾy-i shakhsi]. I am very thankful to God that my dear Surur is well-formed [arasteh] from all aspects and I will always be in love with and enamored of her [ʿashiq and maftun].

Later in the same letter, apparently in response to her insinuation that he must have a maîtresse in Europe with whom he corresponds, he writes:

> I have to tell you that, first, I am a lazy person; that I write to my dear Surur every day, is exceptional, and is because of how much I love her. Second, beyond all else, I hope that we have friendship [rifaqat] between us and thus not hide anything from each other. If there were such a thing, I would be the first person to tell you. I am not going to say that I have never had such correspondence with Farang. To the contrary, I do have some correspondence with Farang acquaintances, but from about a year and a half, two years ago all such correspondence has been discontinued. . . . Currently, except for thinking of Surur, except for Surur's love, except for desiring to see Surur, there is nothing else in my imagination [khiyal].

The invocation of love, affection, and friendship — 'ishq, muhibbat, and rifaqat — seems to have been critical to the changing sensibilities and expectations with regards to conjugal relations. In the early nineteenth century, 'ishq was largely located in classical male-male eros and in the related domain of sufi love and gazing practices. Love/'ishq, friendship/*dusti*, sexual pleasure/*tamattu'*, and forming a family/*ta'ahhul* had distinct domains and separate chapters in books of ethics and advice. Love was certainly not located in the domains of sexual pleasure and forming a family; though in actual life, in a good marriage, affection was expected to develop between husband and wife. At the same time, the distinction among these concepts may also give us an understanding of the implicit expectation, particularly among women, that a marriage based on affection and friendship, if not on flaming love, would be monogamous.

Love and Monogamy

In most of the popular fiction of the period, "monogamy" was an absent term. Nonetheless, as the idea of love-based marriage gained its dominance, it seems that marriage was taken to be self-evidently monogamous; at least that seems to have been women's presumption.[55] They may not have expected sexual monogamy, but they expected conjugal monogamy.[56] This was surely what Fari and her generation had presumed. How had this come about?

To understand the assumed monogamy of love-based marriage, at least among women, one needs to pay closer attention to the language through which these concepts were articulated in the early twentieth century: 'ishq/

love, muhibbat/deep affection, and rifaqat/friendship. We see a glimpse of affection from some early letters between husbands and wives. By the early twentieth century, a different sentiment is expressed through letters between husbands and wives, and occasionally in nonmarried couples' correspondences.

In Taymurtash's letters, for instance, it is striking that wherever he is warding off Surur al-Saltaneh's suspicions of his other possible liaisons, he consistently invokes the classical concept of love and the familiar adage that two loves cannot fit in one heart as two kings cannot occupy the same kingdom. He outdoes that adage by insisting, at times, that even if the other impossible classical duality (two kings in one kingdom) would be possible, there is no way that two loves could occupy the same heart—definitely not his heart, which is fully occupied by her love. But when he discusses his hopes for their conjugal life together, he combines love with affection and friendship.

In *Tihran-i makhauf*, both Mahin and Farrukh use "'ishq" and "dust dashtan" interchangeably over and over. The latter expression combines "dust," or friend, with a verb to make it "to love." ("Dust dashtan" could also mean "to like," but in the context of the novel's conversations and statements, it means "to love.") With the overlap between "friend" and "to love," one could imagine "dust dashtan" worked to cement marital love to a concept closer to friendship.

Shaykh Ibrahim Zanjani, in his memoirs, makes a distinction between affection and love as well. Zanjani equates love with the lustful infatuation "a young bachelor" experiences toward women—indeed, quite close to how Hijazi presents the destructive love in his fiction, which he associates with the desire for sexual pleasure. For Zanjani, love "is totally different from familial affection and marital sharing of life and participating in the affection for a home and children."[57]

Two loves may not fit in one heart, at the same time perhaps, but the other two sentiments, affection and friendship, surely did not demand singularity. One could have multiple relations of affection and friendship. Indeed, the latter two sentiments were seen as the most appropriate for informing the new conjugally centered marital relationships, and that seems to have informed marital practices of some of the men of these generations, including my father, 'Abbas, who loved and married two women, and Taymurtash, who, in addition to Surur al-Saltaneh, took two other wives. He married Tatiyana Markariyan on 8 June 1925, and he married another woman when he was visiting Mashhad in 1931.[58]

If an educated woman's concept of love-based marriage was indeed mediated through romantic fiction, perhaps it was the cultural transplantation/translation of modern love as 'ishq and the latter's classical Perso-Islamic association with singularity (that two loves cannot fit in one heart) that went into women's expectation of monogamy in love-based marriage. Motlagh extends this expectation to "sexual monogamy." It is not clear whether women ever expected sexual monogamy on the part of their husbands; however, many seem to have assumed conjugal monogamy, as my mother, Fari, had, despite her suspicion of 'Abbas's other possible sexual liaisons. For women, a conjugally centered family could not have two centers at once.

For a somewhat later generation of upper-class, urban, young women (and men), coming of age in the late 1930s into the 1940s, the increasing culture of cinemagoing and watching romantic melodramas—a practice that was part of exercising a modern manner of gender-mixing leisure—further consolidated the growing imperial power of love.

Giti Afruz's diaries indicate that when she was in middle school (or what was called "First Cycle," for the seventh to ninth grades), her days were dominated by listening to the radio and reading newspapers and books, including romances.[59] In her high school years (the "Second Cycle," or tenth to twelfth grades), the favorite pastime of Giti and her female friends gradually shifted to going to romantic movies.[60] In the third book of her diaries, Giti discusses one film, *Back Street*, at more length and in terms of her concept of love.[61] She first describes it as a "very beautiful film. It was about a true and forever love, it was deeply sad and we all cried." Several entries later, writing about a heated discussion about the film with one of her friends who had thought the film was terrible nonsense, Giti writes, "To the contrary, it was very good; . . . [T]his was my ideal film. . . . I wish I would have a forever love [*ishq-i abadi*]. This doesn't mean that I won't marry and have kids, but I really want to be in true love with someone to the last minute of my life. This is how this film was for me." Remarkably, she distinguishes between the sentiment of true love, which she desires beyond all else, and the pragmatics of life: getting married and having children, which she doesn't seem to think would be associated with true love. At times, it reads as if Giti is in love with the idea of having a forever love.

Sigheh and Other Secrets

While monogamy as a presumed part of love-based marriage was absent from men's writings (and at times their practices), savage criticism of sigheh marriage was ubiquitous in the press and in fiction. In the genre of morality fiction, prostitutes were often initially sigheh wives.[62] In critical press, sigheh marriage was not only one instance of the terrible marriage practices in Iran, but also quintessentially identified with abuses of Islamic law by unconscionable men. Very quickly, it acquired its dominant marking among modernists, continued into the present, as a legal veneer for prostitution.[63] As Shahla Haeri notes, "Despite its legal and religious legitimacy, it has been culturally marginalized and stigmatized in Persia, and contemptuously dismissed as legalized prostitution by the more secular and modernized Iranian middle classes. Its practitioners often keep their temporary marriages secret, even after the Revolution of 1979, and the regime's attempt to rehabilitate the institution."[64]

Seen as an exchange of sex for money, it surely had nothing to do with the conjugal, love-centered marriage that was being advocated. Sigheh became the easiest and most self-evident foil of evilness for the goodness of love-centered marriage and its associated monogamy.

While the reform press focused on polygyny, sigheh, and other male prerogatives in marriage, and the new fiction was narratively driven by individual choice clashing with parental prerogatives, depicting occasionally good love but largely warning against its terrible destructive consequences, readers would be reading about both. In their reception, the effect of these separate domains coalesced into the generation of a tightly knit set of ideas, with the self-evident goodness of some and the self-evident evilness of others regenerating each other.

Within a single generation, at least for a section of the urban, educated middle class, bigamy (and temporary marriages) had become an embarrassment, if not shameful; it had remained (and remains) legal but had to be practiced as surreptitiously as possible.[65] The multiplicity of wives, even after their divorce or death, has become so thoroughly reprehensible that a 2014 regulation, issued by the Identity Documents Office of the National Registration of Life Events Organization, allows that if a person has divorced his wife, with registration of a second marriage, he can request the elimination of the first wife from his identity booklet. Similarly, he can remove a first wife if she has passed away. In effect, this is the ultimate bureaucratic measure to camouflage previous marriages (ending in divorce or death) and provide a le-

FIGURE 1.1. Cartoon about bigamy laws. Source: *Shargh*, 24 September 2014, p. 16.

gal alibi for a man to look monogamous for all his life.[66] A cartoon published in the daily newspaper *Shargh* satirized the new regulation (see fig. 1.1). A man shows his identity booklet to a woman, saying that he has not married before and that only her name shows up. The woman responds by asking from where, then, he has brought the children named in his booklet. Does he want to claim that he downloaded them?

It was not shameful or secret for earlier generations. A survey of the Najmabadi genealogy—going back to the family patriarch, Baqir (d. ca. 1747, an ironsmith from the village of Najmabad, near Qazvin)—indicates that Baqir's two sons and the Najmabadi men into the next two generations married multiple wives, some simultaneously, some sequentially.[67] Women, after the death of their husbands, often married a husband's brother; two sisters marrying two brothers was not uncommon. Yet with almost no exception, a man in the next generation (that is, of my father, 'Abbas) married only one wife, or only sequentially another wife. The generational shift to monogamy is rather startling. 'Abbas was one of two bigamous exceptions—no wonder he kept it out of the Najmabadi clan's eyes and ears!

This ideational transformation produced secret families and rumored scandals—even to the present moment. When one of the Najmabadi men recently took a second wife, even I, thousands of miles away, became privy to the rumors. It came as no surprise that on a visit to a relative in Tehran in the summer of 2015, when talking about my father's second wife, the conversation immediately took a turn to the Najmabadi men's marital lives and this recent marriage in particular. After an oft-repeated disavowal of gossip (I do apologize, I am not a rude uncultivated [bi-adab] person, God forgive me, I don't say bad things about anyone, but . . .) she went straight to the point: "He married a very young woman a couple of years ago; his [first, non-Muslim] wife had been so loyal to him, she even converted to Islam, his wife for fifty years, taking care of his mother through years of illness, then you go and marry this woman who was your office assistant?" Was it the second marriage as such that had become a family scandal? Was it a class scandal? I had already heard from other family members that his second wife's father was a "mere neighborhood carpenter." Was it an age-inappropriate marriage? The woman was said to have been younger than his children. This was evidently a scandal on several fronts. Shortly after the marriage, he moved out of the Najmabadi neighborhood to a different part of Tehran.

The shamefulness of bigamy also generated a culture of respectability of silence. When I first learned about my father's second family, and that he had kept it a secret from my mother, my reaction was "how unfair." Fairness referenced choice; by not telling my mother, I felt, he had deprived her of getting a divorce, if she so wanted. I speculated that keeping it a secret was his selfish decision: knowing that she may get a divorce, and possibly get to keep the children, under the circumstances of his bigamy, he wanted to avoid losing his kids. But many relatives saw it very differently. They suggested that he had wanted to protect my mother from being hurt and that showed his love and respect for her. Respect became a puzzling, recurrent theme. A cousin said that when my mother had told her about the second marriage, and had asked her why she thought he had kept it hidden, her response had been that not telling her meant that my father held her in respect and had made it possible for her to live in respect.

Respect puzzled me. It assumed that the second marriage, beyond any other injury, humiliated the first wife. Ignorance of it protected my mother; she could continue to keep her head up, so to speak, and people around her would not scold her for staying in a shameful bigamous marriage, or consider the second marriage a sign of her inadequacy as a wife. This is indeed how one relative, Kaukab, put it in reference to her own marriage. Her husband had married "a house servant in a temporary marriage" — the lower-class designation and the despised temporary marriage were common ways of degrading such wives; who else but a servant would be willing to become a mut'a wife? This marriage in fact predated hers. By the time she found out, they had three children (in addition, he already had a daughter and a son from the first marriage). Kaukab had taken this as a severe affront to herself and to her mother: when his family had come to ask for her hand, her mother had made them swear on the Qur'an that their son had no other wife. How did she react? I asked. She pretended ignorance of the first marriage (*beh ru-yi khaudam nayavardam*). It would have been disrespectful otherwise. Another relative practiced ignorance even when "everyone talked" all around her.

My maternal grandmother and her generation may have been deeply upset by their husbands' new marriages, as it is said she had been, but would not have received it as a slight, a humiliation. By her daughter's generation, not only had it become shameful, at times scandalous, for the man to openly marry a second wife but it had also become a disrespectful, humiliating act toward the first wife. At issue, then, was not that not knowing (or the desire not to know) was necessarily, or in the first place, as I had thought, a desire to protect oneself from facing a difficult "choice": divorce or remain with one's children. Rather, not knowing (and pretending not to know) protected one from humiliation, enabling the woman to keep her head up in public.

The triumph of the ideational dominance of love-based marriage is at times indicated by a later generation's recasting of their parents' marriage as a love marriage. Mihrangiz Mallah's narrative of her parents' marriage is one such narrative transformation. Her mother, Khadijeh Afzal Vaziri (b. 1890/1891, d. 1980/1981), the younger of the two daughters of Bibi Khanum Astarabadi and Musa Khan Vaziri, was an accomplished, educated, young woman, working as a teacher both at her mother's school and later at her sister's school, when her mother's brother asked for her hand for his son, Aqa Buzurg. Mother and daughter were against this marriage. Aqa Buzurg was said to be a spoiled, uneducated son; he already had two wives and three children. After five years of her brother's persistence, Bibi Khanum finally bent to familial filial pressure and agreed to the match, despite her daughter's wishes and the disapproval of several other relatives. Aqa Buzurg and his family lived in Naukandeh, in Anzan (in Mazandaran Province). They were local khans, embedded in a vast tribal network, with much landed property to manage. The young urbanite woman spent the first year of her marriage (1914–1915) at her parental home in Tehran before joining her husband in Naukandeh. Her travails of the journey, her hostile reception by her mother-in-law and other local relatives, and her being made fun of because of her differing habits of life are wittily described in her text.[68] She was determined to make things work against all odds, to find ways of *sakhtan* (meaning both to put up with and to build), considering failure dishonorable.[69] Her frequent, complicated pregnancies, and losses of children at childbirth or to sickness, continued to make her marital life a challenge — again narrated in colorful, often funny, detail in her text. Recounting all these years' events in the 1974 interview with her son, Afzal Vaziri's dominant narrative of her marriage coheres with her generation's concept and practices: marriages were largely for forming a family and attending to one's children. In the best cases, affectionate bonds would develop between spouses as an effect of years of living together; emotional investment remained largely with one's own female kin and friends and with one's children.

At times, however, with all her wit and determination to make things work, she despaired, considering her husband the source of all her pains.[70] At times, Afzal Vaziri even welcomed a possible death during childbirth.[71] After ten years of living in Mazandaran, suffering from health complications and frequent pregnancies, she took her four surviving children and moved to Tehran. Over the next years, she accompanied her husband to several other cities, but when he decided to take up a position back in the Gurgan area, and her old asthma troubles recurred in more severe form, she returned to Tehran for good, now with five children.[72] During this absence, her husband took a sigheh wife, Nusrat Zaman. They had one daughter, Guli. After Nusrat Zaman's sigheh with Aqa Buzurg ended, she married Mr. Parvin. Upon this marriage, Guli was brought to Afzal Vaziri's home and integrated into her household.[73]

Pressed by her daughter Mahlaqa, Afzal Vaziri had spoken of the sentiment of sakhtan that defined her approach to her marriage. When speaking about her own antipathy toward men and marriage, Mahlaqa Mallah offered as one reason the fact that her mother was also "anti-men" (anti-*mard*) and was forced to marry Mahlaqa's father and suffered and put up with him for a lifetime.[74] She recalled, when she was very young, that one day she was sewing a dress for a new servant, a young woman they had recently hired. Her father, sitting across from her on the other side of a *korsi* (a type of low table), approached her and asked her to make the dress very pretty. This made Mahlaqa deeply angry. She screamed at her father to get out of her sight, then ran to her mother and asked why she had put up with this man for all these years, suffering so much at his hand. Her mother, according to Mahlaqa, responded, "So that *you* wouldn't have to suffer indignities [*ta tau tusari nakhauri*]." Mahlaqa went on to expand that as the oldest child she had reached a comprehension of how her mother had suffered and put up with her father, in silence (*dar sukut tahammul kard*).[75]

This marriage was then anything but a love marriage. The sentiment of an unsuitable arranged marriage between vastly different cousins — described in Afzal Vaziri's narrative as a match between a spoiled, uneducated son of a tribal chief, brought up in the rural hinterlands of Mazandaran, with herself, as an accomplished, educated, young, urban woman — is echoed (with much flourish) in the initial pages of the chapter titled "Marriage" in Mihrangiz Mallah's ventriloquizing of her mother.[76] Yet, in a few short pages, in the next chapter, "Mazandaran," it becomes a romantic sad drama, with no referentiality to the original text: "But at night, when I had to share my love with others, when a sorrow would sink into my innermost parts, and would bring tears into my eyes, things were different. Each night, it was a different wife's turn and my husband was in another bed. Each time that it was one of my co-wives' [*havu-ha*] turn, that night, alone in my room, my eyes were focused on stars until a cloud would block my eyes and I would realize a puddle of tears had formed on my pillow and tears have clouded my vision. I would empty the puddle with my hands, until it would fill up again, or else I would fall asleep."[77] And there follows a didactic discourse on women's oppression, also not in the original. Indeed, throughout the edited version, transcription of Afzal Vaziri's witty oral narrative has become a didactic dramatic text, as if a school composition (*insha'*).

While novels, newspapers, and later films, as well as what one heard about marriage in Europe or read in accounts of those who had spent time in Europe, provided some of the media through which the ideas of love-based marriage and conjugally centered family gained power, one can also trace through other material objects the growing presence of these ideas in daily life. Among these, photographs, wedding outfits, and letters of affection provide further insight, as the next chapter will discuss.

2. Objects

Letters, Wedding Clothes, and Photographs

Letters of Affection

Changes in the idea of a good marriage and the desire for such marriages seem to have been not only linked with changing reading habits but also accompanied by different writing practices. As we already saw in the case of Surur al-Saltaneh and Taymurtash, writing love/loving letters seems to have gained popularity. Several family collections in the Women's Worlds in Qajar Iran (WWQI) digital archive (www.qajarwomen.org) include a substantial body of such letters. Some were between contracted couples (*'aqdi*), before their ceremonial wedding (*'arusi*) — for example, those of Surur al-Saltaneh and 'Abd al-Husayn Taymurtash. Some were between married couples separated for various reasons, including husbands assigned to serve in a different part of the country and the wife staying with her own family (as in the case of my parents, Fari and 'Abbas, and of Shams al-Muluk 'Azudi and her husband, Hisam al-Dawleh), or husbands going abroad for education or medical treatment (as documented in A'zam al-Saltaneh and Nusrat al-Saltaneh's letters). Some letters are between unrelated men and women and would fit closer with the romantic love letters genre, such as Badr al-Muluk and Amin al-Sultan's letters, and there are several letters whose writers and receivers so far have remained unidentified.[1] Similarly, in her memoir Mahin Banu reports of a flaming love that her father had developed for Qamar al-Saltaneh:

> Shazdeh jan [Nuzhat al-Saltaneh, Muzaffar al-Din shah's wife] had a cousin, Qamar al-Saltaneh who later on married Haji Nasir al-Saltaneh Diba. She would visit us with her mother. Her mother was very beautiful. My father had seen Qamar al-Saltaneh from behind a glass window and fell in love with her. Not just ordinary love, deeply in love; he used to write long love poems for her, they would put the sheets of paper in

a sack and tie it around my neck to take to school. My mother would tie the sack herself. Very strange that she accepted her husband to be in love with Qamar al-Saltaneh. . . . Qamar al-Saltaneh had been in marriage contract ['aqd] with a Mr. Banki; when she sees him at the 'aqd, she doesn't like him and says "I don't want to marry him." It took five years before Banki agreed to a divorce. These love correspondences belonged to this period.[2]

In later decades, writing and exchanging love letters seems to have become part of the emerging street-socializing practices for women of leisured classes. At times, one side of the correspondence is unidentified, such as in several letters written by an unidentified woman to Mahdiquli Mirza Nusrat Muzaffari. We have more of the letters written by men and saved by women; women's letters, in particular those of wives to their husbands, were either not kept, have been lost, or remain inaccessible. Shams al-Muluk's letters to her husband are unusual in this regard.

What these letters, despite many differences, contributed to was a culture of conjugality of the couple. The growing literacy among urban middle-class women made these letters more private and individual, but illiteracy was not an insurmountable obstacle; scribes, public or private, acted as intermediaries. That mediation, however, took away moments of privacy. In one letter from Nusrat al-Saltaneh to A'zam al-Saltaneh, he writes that he very much desired to write the kind of nonsense talk between a wife and a husband (*muhmalat va muzakhrafat-i zan-shauhari*), but he is concerned that the letters will be read by others and, of course, that would not be a good and respectable thing (*az adab kharij ast va khub nist*): "God willing, we will talk such nonsense when we are together."[3] Perhaps this type of communication also was an incentive to learn to write. That seems to have been the case for A'zam al-Saltaneh, who was learning to write during the period of their correspondence and at times would write in her own handwriting—occasions that were received warmly and encouragingly by her husband: "I received the letter that you had written in your own dear hand-writing. I swear on your life, on Mu'in [their son]'s life, I was so delighted that, mash'allah, you have succeeded to write a letter in your own hand-writing. You have truly worked hard and thank God you have reached this point. The rest will be easy. In-sha'allah, for this achievement, I will bring you a good prize."[4]

These letters often located the letter writers within the larger kinship network in which they were embedded. Nonetheless, written from one spouse to the other, a letter also mediated and generated a particular style of affectionate conjugality. Whether the marriage was arranged by families (as most likely was the case with Surur al-Saltaneh, Shams al-Muluk, and A'zam al-Saltaneh); initiated through a meeting of the couple outside familial circuits, as was the case with my aunt and uncle, 'Isa and 'Iffat; or introduced through familial circuits but pursued directly, as was the case with my parents, Fari and 'Abbas, couples writing affectionate letters to each other cultivated conjugalization of marriage and emphasized affectionate companionship as its meaning.

Letter writing as a mode of cultivating friendship was, of course, nothing new. What we see in the couples' letters, however, was cultivation of a different sentiment. At times, it was the language of romance, as in many of the "love letters" on the wwqi site. But in the case of the conjugal couple, it was cultivation of deep affection — the word most frequently used in these letters was muhibbat, not 'ishq — informing the relationship between a (future) married couple.[5] This language they shared with some of the earlier husband-wife letters, perhaps even going back to Qa'im Maqam's letters to his wife, Shahzadeh Khanum Kuch (sent from Mashhad to Tabriz), or with the more contemporary Shaykh al-Islam of Qazvin in his correspondence with his wives, Sakineh Khanum, Rukhsareh Khanum, and Farah al-Saltaneh.

And yet conjugal couples' letters did not all do the same affective work. Some, such as those between Nusrat al-Saltaneh and A'zam al-Saltaneh, were written when they had already been married for a long time and had three children; what is noteworthy in their case is the possibly new manner of writing letters home from Europe, to *all* significant family members. Nusrat al-Saltaneh writes to his mother, his wife, and occasionally to his children. In these letters, he is a son, a husband, and a father. In this sense, the letters are not as much generating conjugality of the couple as indicating the important place of the conjugal bond, next to maternal-son and paternal-children relationships.

In the letters to his wife, Nusrat al-Saltaneh uses contemporary conventional language of love and adoration, at times stock phrases, but also often talks about their relationship as one that had matured over many years. According to family lore, he was very much in love with his wife and remained enamored of her. Unusual among his cohort of princes, he remained monogamous all his life.[6] He often complains that A'zam al-Saltaneh did not write to him often enough, and he repeatedly asks if she no longer loved him. In one letter, he writes that they had grown old and must love each other even more, and that the more time passed the more he loved her.

Shams al-Muluk 'Azudi and Hisam al-Dawleh's letters, as well as those exchanged between Surur al-Saltaneh and 'Abd al-Husayn Taymurtash, and 'Abbas and Fari, all belong to the initial period of their marriages, at times between 'aqd (the contractual marriage) and 'arusi (the ceremonial wedding). They are pre-cohabitation courting letters. Haj 'Izz al-Mamalik Ardalan, in his memoirs, writes that once he and his future wife were contractually married, over the following two to three months, he sent her love letters (*kaghazha-yi 'ashiqaneh*) and she wrote back friendly responses (*javab-i dustaneh*).[7] The interval between 'aqd and 'arusi, especially among upper classes and especially if one or both members of the contractually married couple were underage, could be months, at times years, to permit appropriate preparation for an eventual cohabitation as husband and wife. Such postponement could also be occasioned by reluctance of one side to consummate the marriage or by unavoidable circumstances, such as a husband's travels.

Shams al-Muluk 'Azudi and Hisam al-Dawleh were cousins. Both were from prominent Qajar families. Shams al-Muluk was the daughter of Fakhr al-Dawleh and Nusrat Allah Khan Amir A'zam (1878–1916). Hisam al-Dawleh was a grandson of Bahram Mirza (himself a grandson of Fath'ali Shah). More significantly for our story, Shams al-Muluk, her sister Fakhr al-Muluk, and their younger brother Yad Allah had all been home-tutored by Hisam al-Dawleh, including in the French language. In her letters to Hisam al-Dawleh, Shams al-Muluk occasionally writes a few lines in French. She refers to her father as Papa. This seems to have been the period when "Papa" and "Maman" entered the Persian language. Perhaps the tutoring sessions were also the space in which they had developed an affection for each other.

Early in their marriage, in 1913–1914, when Shams al-Muluk's father was based in Shahrud as its governor, the couple lived apart. Amir A'zam had taken his family, including his recently married daughter, with him against her and her husband's protestations. He was, he had said, dependent on his daughter for his house management. Shams al-Muluk and Hisam al-Dawleh wrote letters to each other systematically; she numbers her letters to him and from these, it is clear that he did the same. He saved some of her letters in an envelope and later gave them to their daughter Nuzhat al-Zaman.[8] We do not have his letters to her.

The language of Shams al-Muluk's letters is deeply affectionate (she mentions muhibbat and *mihr* [fondness]), often centered on the pain of their separation (*mufariqat*), his insistence (as reported by her) that she would join him in Tehran, and her explanation that unless her Papa would grant her permission, despite her intense desire, she could not do so. Even in the French segments, she uses adore, *aimé*, but not *amour*. Occasionally, she does use a language of love in Persian, as when she writes, in letter number 9 of 13 Rajab (1332?/7 June 1914), "alas the path of union [*visal*] of these two poor lovers ['ashiq] has been blocked by short-sightedness and heartlessness of Papa, and it is totally unclear when this separation will come to an end." She prays that soon God will bring the two sincere lovers together.

The letters are from a wife to her husband, an exercise in conjugality. Yet their conjugality is at the same time cultivated through recalling their former relationship as tutor and student. As her former tutor, Hisam al-Dawleh continues to be interested in his wife's education. In response to his query about her daily program, in letter number 9, she reports that "we have three hours of Arabic tutoring, and in the evenings two hours of French, . . . and Arithmétique [written in French] and Récitation [written in French] have now been added, . . . also some practicing of piano." She expresses delight in her education. Through her voice as a student reporting to her former tutor/current husband, a new conjugal bond consolidates itself through narration of the old tutor-student relationship, carrying into their conjugality a sense of a respectful teacher-student, husband-wife hierarchy.

As we already saw, Surur al-Saltaneh and Taymurtash did not begin to cohabit immediately either. Their wedding festivities had to wait for over a year. In the meantime, Taymurtash visited his bride occasionally and wrote letters in between visits, even though for much of the period they were living in the same city. These were uncertain times, especially for a politically ambitious civil servant such as Taymurtash. After the restoration of the Constitutional government in mid-July 1909, very possibly he went back to Khurasan and successfully worked to get elected from that province to the second Majlis, which was inaugurated on 14 November 1909. He seemed to have rented a place near the parliament building—he says in one letter that except for Mondays and Fridays, he had to be there every day and all day. He lived a relatively modest life and did not consider his place worthy of his bride; he had married "up."[9]

Upon marriage to Surur al-Saltaneh, Taymurtash began looking for an appropriate residence to rent and furnish before he could ask her family to agree to set the date for a proper wedding. Finding the right house in Tehran seemed to be anything but easy: a situation that at times gave rise to tension between the couple, as reflected in their correspondence.

He was eager to see his bride and see her often, but even though he was contractually married to Surur al-Saltaneh, he could visit her only occasionally; she was living in her paternal residence. Since her mother had passed away when she was young, her paternal aunt Nayyir Qudsiyeh seems to have taken over her growing up. The visits were highly regulated and closely supervised: she first had to grant him a visitation date, presumably with permission of the house elders; they were seldom left totally alone. In one of the letters he wrote to her after such a visit, he laments his departure time and how "Mameh Khanum, Zahra Sultan, and Ruqiyeh Baji kept saying my time was over and I had to leave." Writing flamingly passionate letters between two visits became his way of keeping the marriage alive. He profusely professed his unfailing love and passion in sentence after sentence, letter after letter. She reciprocated by writing back, though never often enough and affectionate enough to stop his incessant complaints. She wrote kind words; he wrote fiery passion. For a brief period in December 1909, he returned to Mashhad to deal with supervising his family property. A couple of letters were exchanged from that distance; he found the separation insufferably hard. He rushed back to Tehran not only to be closer to his love, but for political reasons as well. In one letter, he noted that not being in Majlis could have negative consequences, as Asif al-Dawleh was dismissed (from his governorship of Fars) when he had refused to appear in Majlis. At the time of his return to Tehran, his father had been ill; shortly after, he received news of his death. This further pushed back the possibility of their wedding. They finally got married in April (or May) 1910.

Compared with 'Abbas's letters to Fari in 1941–1943, these letters similarly cultivated conjugal affection at a time of distance. Despite that commonality, they are somewhat distinct in prose, expressed sentiment, and cultural affect. There are some obvious differences of social status (the couples discussed here belonged to Qajar court circles and urban high notables) and a time interval of three to four critical decades. These were decades in which Persian prose writing took an increasing distance from the classical, more ornate prose of earlier times; it came closer to conversational Persian, in part through writings of people like Nizam Vafa ('Abbas's adored teacher), in part through the press (the increase in the number and readership of newspapers), and, of course, through novels. Young, educated urban women were avid readers and letter writers.

As Dena Goodman has suggested in a different context, quoting from a letter exchanged between two young female friends, "'In finding between us a distance that could not be crossed easily, the need to write to each other made itself felt almost at the moment when we began to care about each other.' . . . Letter writing was not auxiliary to friendship; it was the matrix and the medium in which friendship developed."[10] In the case of married couples, their letters were the medium through which conjugality was cultivated.

A whole stack of letters, written over the first year of my parents' marriage, when 'Abbas, working for the Ministry of Agriculture, was posted first to Gurgan, and later to Saveh, Kirman, and Bandar 'Abbas, has recorded the early love years.

In September 1941, my father had been in Gurgan, on the eastern coast of the Caspian Sea, when the Allied forces invaded Iran. The northern provinces were occupied by the Soviet Army; the south, by the British. He left his post and came to Tehran, hoping he would not have to return to a zone of occupation and could get repositioned in Tehran. That is when in a visit to his uncle 'Isa, he met Fari and began courting her. Having failed to get a repositioning, in December 1941, he went back to Gurgan, now trying even harder, mobilizing all his local connections, to declare his work in the area completed. The first letters to Fari were sent from there. Four sets of letters, covering 1 December to 9 December 1941, date from this period of premarital courtship. Compared to the letters he wrote after their wedding, the language of these letters is deeply affectionate but respectfully polite. He addresses her as "my loving Fari" (*Fari-yi mihrabanam*); he begs her to convince his uncle 'Isa to make preparations for their 'aqd when he returns to Tehran, hopefully by mid-December; he is concerned that their courtship has become subject of "people's talk," and he fears such talk. There is an indication that his own supportive uncle 'Isa was resisting such a fast marriage. At the time, the employment future of his nephew was unclear; either he would become unemployed (if he left his post in Gurgan) or Fari's marriage would start as a long-distance marriage. Neither option was considered desirable. 'Abbas writes that Fari should explain to his uncle that he had enough savings for the wedding and that his uncle should stop worrying about his employment outlook. His uncle must make these preparations at once "because I love you." Reading these words, Fari had underlined them with a pencil. But when? Upon her first reading, with a smile of a beloved's satisfaction on her face, or after 1987, with painful tears in her eyes? The penciled underlining showed signs of trembling, so I was inclined to believe the latter.

The uncertainty of the war and Allied occupation, and 'Abbas's unclear job prospects were not the only issues making Fari's family cautious about a quick match. 'Abbas's mother and other Najmabadis were against this marriage. Compared to some of her other sisters, Fari's marriage to 'Abbas—despite the title *muhandis* (engineer) he had earned upon graduating from Karaj Agricultural College—would have been received "by people who talked" as marrying inappropriately, perhaps "down." All worked against the match. One sister, Gawhar al-Muluk, for instance, had married 'Adil al-Dawleh Javan, a nationally known and respected judge, who served in the judiciary, including as attorney general in several provinces. Another sister, Fakhr al-Muluk, had married Dr. Isma'il Baygi, a university professor and the future president of Mashhad University. In several of 'Abbas's later (postmarriage) letters, he returns to this issue repeatedly: the difficulties they had to suffer being far and away from each other, and his working in trying conditions away from Tehran, were necessary so that he could save a lot of money and so that Fari could hold her head up and live as good a life as her sisters. He would beg her again and again, when she complained about their separation, to learn patience (*saburi*) from her oldest sister, Badi' al-Muluk.

Beyond the concern for people talking about them and 'Abbas's urgent pleas for consolidating the new relationship through the performance of the marriage contract, these early letters continued the work of initial months of long-distance courtship: she had apparently given him a book to read, perhaps some sort of a romance novel as indicated by a few phrases he copied from the book into one of the letters. He does not seem to quite like it, finds it good for "children" (meaning very young people), not for them who are seriously committed to a life together. He suggests that Fari should read Nizam Vafa's book, "which is a book of affection [muhibbat], something of which I was then deprived." Possibly this was *Amaj-i dil* (The heart's targets), published in 1935. Both Nizam Vafa and affection are recurring topics in many future letters. In several letters, he writes short fables from Nizam Vafa that he had either heard or read. The two books he took with him on his work trips in this period were one of Nizam Vafa's and the Qur'an. In one letter, describing a day's activity, he writes that he read some Nizam Vafa, some Qur'an, and then thought a lot about his Fari.

'Abbas had been a student of Nizam Vafa's during his three years at the Agricultural College. By all accounts, Nizam Vafa, who after several years of political activity as a Constitutionalist, dedicated the last four decades of his life to teaching and developed very affectionate bonds with his students. Many have written in their memoirs how they found solace in his writings. He has been called a "poet of the heart" whose poetry had a calming effect. He taught both at the high school level, to boys and girls, and at the Agricultural College. Some of his students went on to become educators, and schools in several cities were named after him. A whole generation of urban, educated men and women were his students; many became his friends for life. The dominant themes running through his poetry often have to do with love and pain (familiar themes in Persian poetry), but with a bent toward dusti (friendship) and muhibbat (deep affection) rather than passionate love ('ishq). 'Abbas highlights these themes in his references to the writer. The close friendships he made in his college years and later at work, with Karim Sa'i (1910–1952), Yadollah Yazdaniyan (1909–2001), and Ibrahim Mu'ini (1913–2010) were lifelong friendships. With the latter two, they became family friendships.

Muhibbat was also the dominant term that 'Abbas used in his letters: it was how he wrote about his feelings not only for Fari—for whom he did use the more intense vocabulary of 'ishq (passionate love) and *parastish* (adoration)—but more significantly for the relationships he developed in the first year of their marriage with Fari's sisters and mother. This is the period that his ties with his own family, except with his father and a relative-friend, were virtually nonexistent. After they were married in January 1942, when in Tehran in between out-of-Center (*kharij az markaz*) assignments, he would stay at the house where 'Isa, 'Iffat, Khanum jun, and Fari lived. This house often had additional occupants: sometimes, Fari's oldest sister, Badi' al-Muluk (who was estranged from her husband), stayed there with her young son Khusrau, days at a time; and another sister, Latifeh Khanum, who, when she was between job assignments to various cities, joined the household with her two daughters, Qamar and Huma. When Latifeh married for the second time and lived in Qum and later in Bandar 'Abbas (where her new husband had been posted), Qamar moved to Tehran and lived there. Within this crowded and changing household, 'Abbas had become sort of a *damad-i sarkhuneh* (a husband who joins the bride's household)—something he enjoyed. He writes over and over again how Fari's family had become the family he had not experienced, how they had embraced him with the affection he had always desired and of which he had been deprived. But the status of a live-in husband was also something that made him uncomfortable. He saw it as a temporary necessity; he had to work hard and save money to repair his father's old crumbling house and also amend his relations with his side of the family so that once he returned and settled in Tehran, he and Fari could move into his family's house, located in the Najmabadi clan neighborhood. But for the moment, he only spoke in the most negative terms about the Najmabadis; he called them cruel, unloving. He encourages Fari to visit his father (Aqa'i) and cultivate his love. He wrote, in several letters, that "if he takes a liking to you, we will be all set." Unbeknownst to Fari, and something I only found out in my familial detective work some seventy years later, Aqa'i's approval was critical because he had wanted Mansureh Khanum to become 'Abbas's wife. To make it easier for Fari, 'Abbas sends letters for his father to her and asks her to take them over to him. But he instructs her to stay away from all other Najmabadis, including his mother. In one letter, he says that in everything he respects her decision and independence, but on one issue he insists: she is forbidden to socialize with the Najmabadis. Only after she is pregnant (in the summer of 1942) does he suggest that she should begin to visit his mother, but not to get offended if his mother used harsh or cynical language with her. While Fari's visits to her mother-in-law, Nuri Khanum, breaks the ice of boycott (*qahr*), the full mending of the relationship and Nuri Khanum's move into 'Abbas's paternal house awaited her second pregnancy. In her memoirs, Fari mentions that her first child's midwife was not Sadiqeh Khanum (an obstetrician sister of Nuri Khanum's who home-delivered her next two children; her last was a hospital birth); Sadiqeh Khanum had recommended a friend of hers, since at that time, there was still a state of nonrecognition of Fari by Nuri Khanum, and Sadiqeh Khanum had to respect that.

Aside from discussing his work routine, reporting on his persistent attempts to return to Tehran so that they could get married, and referring to the books he read, there is an accounting of mundane daily life activities as a way of recalling his time in Tehran over the previous months. Returning from a public bath, he is "thinking of her and Badi' al-Muluk going to the bath together" and their reported laughter; he hopes they continue to remember him in their outings. He repeatedly asks after Fari's mother and sisters, at times even their dog, Panbeh, saving his warmest greetings for Badi' al-Muluk who had been the most supportive of their marriage even when others, including 'Abbas's own uncle, did not seem to go along. In a later letter, 'Abbas says that he and Fari owed their happiness to Badi' al-Muluk. When discussing a book that she had given him, he says he hopes that they will read and discuss it together once he is back in Tehran. The letters, their writing and reading, act as the continuation of their brief months of premarital courtship, bridging onto their marriage.

The last couple of letters become impatient and despondent: he has written two letters to his uncle begging him to make preparations for their contractual marriage and has received no answer; he has received no letters from her: "what are you doing not writing to me, . . . what a terrible trip this was, what a fate [*qismat*] that I have to be away from the person I love, the days feel so long; today, it has been ten days since I've been away from Tehran, but it feels longer than the thirteen months when I was last away."

Eventually, 'Abbas returns to Tehran, possibly in late December. They get married on 14 January 1942. Despite his attempts to get a job in Tehran, he has to return to the Gurgan area again, shortly after the Iranian new year. For the next many months, they have short periods of togetherness in Tehran, separated by months of being apart: mid-April to mid-June 1942, he is in the Gurgan area; end of July to late September 1942 (with a short ten-day visit to Tehran), in Saveh; and then from late November 1942 to mid-January 1943, in Kirman and Bandar 'Abbas. Much to their mutual distress, on their first anniversary, they could not be together. Instead, upon Fari's initiative, they gave for thanksgiving (*shukraneh*) bread and rice to the poor in the Kirman area—a generally underdeveloped area at the time, near famine caused by the wartime situation. He makes it back before the birth of their first child. In his letters, he had indicated that he wanted their child's name to be inclusive of hers—Farinaz for a girl and Fariburz for a boy. Farinaz was born on 3 February 1943.

The prose and feel of the postmarital letters are somewhat different from the earlier ones; they are more explicitly loving, passionate, occasionally verging on erotica. What they do have in common with the premarital letters is the sense of cultivating a young relationship, interrupted by 'Abbas's departures, through a detailed reporting of banal, everyday life doings: if we cannot become a married couple through actually sharing these ordinary moments of daily life, we will generate that sense of a shared life by writing letters.

The first letter from this period begins with a line of salutations (*salam salam salam* . . . , repeated the whole width of the paper) and a second line of kisses (*bous bous bous* . . . , repeated the whole width of the paper) and, only then, "my dear Fari" (see fig. 2.1). Future letters include more explicit sexualized adorations.

For me, as a reader in 2016, these letters often seem boringly repetitious: page after page, day after day, reporting on his daily life, with occasional novelties. For instance, when 'Abbas went to Turkmen Sahra, he wrote a four-page letter on 29 April 1942 that turns ethnographic:

> *Dear Fari, for today's lunch I am the guest of one of the Turkmen chiefs. I am currently sitting in the alachiq [a large dome-shaped tent, usually covered inside and over the tent with kilims] and want to write to you a bit about their ethics and behavior.*

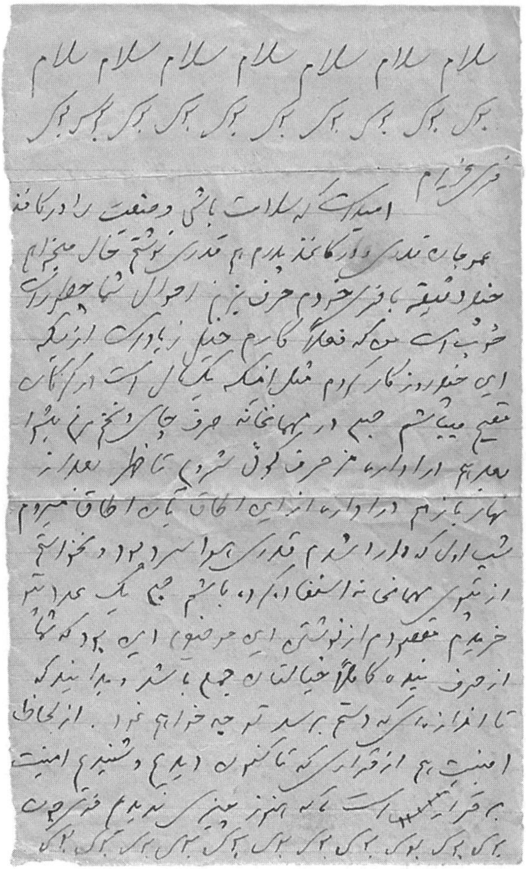

FIGURE 2.1. 'Abbas's letter to Fari. Source: Author's holdings.

In the middle of the alachiq, there is a large tripod that holds the milk cauldron; basically, the kitchen is right in the middle of the alachiq. . . . Behind me facing north . . . is the storage area, containing charcoal, wheat, flour, rice, etc. The area on my right is considered the bedroom. All beddings have been piled up there. The southern part of the alachiq constitutes the place for animals. . . . [T]here is [a] horse harness and bit, as well as some leaves, and the dughskin. A bit further, the older daughter of the chief is sitting, cleaning wool. There is also a teapot and a cup. You must drink the whole teapot. Someone just sharpened a knife and took a poor sheep out to slaughter. They slaughter a whole sheep for a guest . . . this is part of their ethics of hospitality. . . . If someone is passing a Turkmen alachiq and they invite him in, he must get off his horse and come in . . . have some tea or eat some bread with them. . . . I am now waiting to eat a Turkmen dish, chikdarmeh.

Similarly, when he travels to Saveh, he writes about the poverty of the city, expressing his deep distress over conditions of life there. Two pages of a four-page letter, written on 1 August 1942, is devoted to describing the state of the city:

City of Saveh or one of the ruins of Iran, it is a city of beggars. . . . It has one street; coming from Tehran, one enters the street, the two sides of this street are decorated with mounds of dirt and trash, or walls of houses in disrepair. Along this whole street, which is about a thousand meters long, there are four one-storey buildings, made of mud bricks and whitewashed. . . . [T]he city bazaar is about five hundred meters long and four meters wide with several small shops, often empty of goods. Many poor people sit around there. . . . I saw a lot of quarrels among desperate people. . . .

Houses in Saveh are small mud domed shapes, perhaps about two to two and a half meters in diagonal. There are no windows, they have a wooden door; once you close the door it becomes night inside. The door is large so that donkeys and other animals can enter as well. . . . [O]ne in a hundred of these houses is whitewashed. . . . [P]eople are so poor that husband and wife, brother and brother fight over a sheep or some wheat, or a watermelon.

'Abbas's letters are almost like keeping a diary: each letter was often a stack of many pages (in one instance, thirty-one pages, and another time twenty-eight pages). He would write over several days, until the day when the postal service was leaving from his area for Tehran or a traveler was making the journey. He wrote almost every day, at times three times a day (at breakfast, lunch, and dinner—mealtimes that he would have been sharing with Fari if in Tehran), detailing what he had for breakfast, what he did at work, what he cooked for his lunch, when he went back to work, what he cooked for dinner, and so on. From his responses to her letters, Fari seems to have been writing in a similar style. Among her friends at work (at the time, she worked as a typist at the Ministry of Education), two were named frequently, Zinat 'Asgari and Zahra Kia. They apparently teased her for using her breaks to write to him and playfully needled her: What kind of a husband would leave his young, newly married wife behind? At work, when she had no work-related material to type, she translated from French and typed books—a cookbook, with a section of Iranian recipes (fifty-nine typed pages; see figs. 2.2 and 2.3), followed by a section of French recipes (seventy-five pages); a manuscript on nursing instructions (completed in March 1940; see fig. 2.4); and ten pages of other household instructions (ranging from how to set the table to how

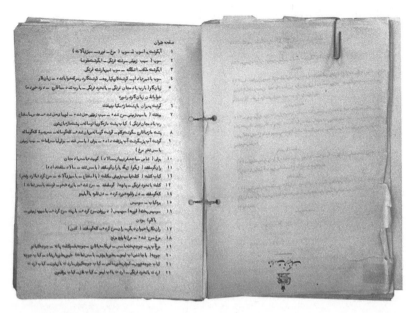

FIGURES 2.2 and 2.3. Table of contents of Fari's cookbook. Source: Author's holdings.

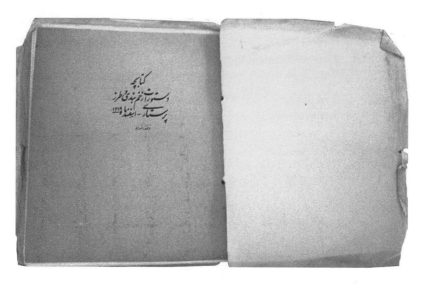

FIGURE 2.4. Cover of Fari's nursing instruction book. Source: Author's holdings.

to clean stains from leather) have remained from these years. In his 29 April 1942 letter, 'Abbas sends her the recipe for the Turkmen dish, chikdirmeh, telling her to add it to her cookbook.

When 'Abbas was assigned north to the Gurgan area, or south to Kirman and Bandar 'Abbas, these were war zones, under Soviet and British occupation, respectively. Fari worried; he reassured her of his well-being. On 8 December 1942, massive demonstrations over bread prices broke out in Tehran in Baharistan Square, in front of the parliament, protesting government inaction. Hearing the news on the radio caused 'Abbas to panic, as Fari's workplace on Shahabad Street was in the same area. He sent two telegrams and over the days that it took to hear back, he organized his affairs to quit his job and return to Tehran. He writes again and again that he will never go away unless he can take her with him. At the end, a telegram of safety did arrive.

Sharing these ordinary, mundane details generated for them a sense of being together, being a married couple. What they could not enact in physical proximity — living these moments together upon their marriage — they lived through these letters. In their totality, the practice of writing to each other generated their coupledom, their conjugality, their being husband and wife together, person to person, each at the same time located within (or, in 'Abbas's case, at the margin of) their respective familial spaces. The letters thus not only positioned them as the conjugal couple they were becoming, despite the miles separating them, but also worked toward positioning the couple within the two familial networks. His place within the Suhrabi family was a negotiation of the warmth and support he had received, but also the pressure of competing with the more established in-laws. He needed to save his own masculine pride by being able to provide Fari with a comparable home and status. When in one letter, she is hesitant to buy shoes she clearly desires, worrying about their finances, he insists that they can afford it, and she should buy them.

Fari's place within his family had to be slowly engineered. 'Abbas instructed her incessantly: go visit my father; I am sending a letter to take to him; happy to hear he laughed with you; if we can keep him happy things will work out; sending a letter for my mother, give it to him to give to her. This last instruction changed once Fari was pregnant. Eventually, Fari reports on visiting Nuri Khanum. At some point she even ends up staying overnight; later when he sends a letter for his mother for her to take, he tells her to give it to her directly, no longer through his father.

Again and again, 'Abbas writes that only their bodies were apart (*jisman*) but never their souls (*ruhan*). When she writes that one of her work friends had teased her, saying, "out of sight, out of heart" (*az dil biravad har ankeh az dideh biraft*), he writes, "That is right, because you have gone from my eyes deep inside me." Writing and reading these seemingly boring, repetitiously detailed daily reports attempted to make up for that bodily apartness and generate intimacies. This is most evident in his writing of imagined embraces, the numerous kisses and other physically intimate gestures he sends in his letters, and her descriptions of his "empty place" in her room in the house

But beyond explicit bodily talk, the very holding of a beloved's letter (a bodily token), the trace of what her and his hand had held and pressed on paper, sustained the young newlywed couple's intimate senses and sutured their coupledom at a critical moment of their lives. Material effects he had cultivated and left behind now stood as he in his absence, in his "empty place," and continued their life in the letters. He had planted several flowerpots, some unfamiliar ones (his specialty in the Agricultural College was botany and cultivation of flowers); she cared for them — that daily care served as his place in her life — reported on their development, and asked for their names. He teased her for her botanical ignorance, when he had once told her the flowering plant he had left her was amaryllis and had no Persian name. She kept referring to it as "that flower pot"; he wrote back saying that he was glad the Persian Academy of Language had assigned "that flower pot" for amaryllis.[11]

With letters, he sent her other material remnants of his days: different wild, dried flowers, at times embedded at the center of a letter or at times at the corner. Fari cut some of the corner pieces and saved them separately (figs. 2.5 – 2.6). At times the letters included loose calendar sheets he had ripped out of a desk calendar, noting on each something about his day and his thought about her on that day (fig. 2.7). All such little objects were material tokens of their having been together, helping them remember that togetherness, and imagining being together again.[12]

Wedding Outfits and Studio Photographs

As Alan Duben and Cem Behar have argued, the entry of European objects of daily use (such as knives and forks, furnishings, etc.) into Ottoman homes, bringing with them new manners of doing things, distanced people from the ways their parents did things, setting in motion "a complex symbolic act laden with various layers of meaning."[13] Often, social histories discuss at length seemingly more important grand changes, under the rubric of modernity, modernization, and the modern individuated self, but tend to ignore the very ordinary processes through which changes in concepts and practices of daily life took shape. Thomas Levin quotes Siegfried Kracauer on "quotidian micrologies" that could be useful to think with: "One must rid oneself of the delusion that it is the major events which have the most decisive influence on people. They are much more deeply and continuously influenced by the tiny catastrophes which make up daily life."[14]

The tiny changes in daily life, and their almost ordinariness, also contribute to the unfinished character of "achieving modernity"; it is never smooth or evenly and homogeneously spread. Modernity is never achieved. As Bruno Latour famously put it: we have never been modern.[15]

Because of the ordinary ways in which, for instance, people begin to use individual eating utensils on individual plates (in place of using one's fingers and eating from a common platter), and because even people who have for several generations eaten with knives and forks still continue at times to eat from a common platter and with their fingers, the very ordinariness of the

FIGURES 2.5 and 2.6.
Pages of letters from
'Abbas to Fari. Figure 2.5
shows embedded dried
flowers, and figure 2.6
shows the corners that
Fari had removed. Source:
Author's holdings.

FIGURE 2.7. A page from 'Abbas's desk calendar. Source: Author's holdings.

shaping of modern individuals through these life habits continues to regenerate totally unmodern or, better yet in Svetlana Boym's expression, off-modern practices as well.[16]

Seemingly ordinary objects of life thus acted as generational markers, signaling the changing meaning of family. They have contributed to the conjugal centeredness of family. The white bridal wedding gown and the dark formal suit of the groom, replacing colorful and often fancily embroidered clothes that brides and grooms used to wear at wedding celebrations, constituted such material objects. Figures 2.8–2.12 reproduce a few from the wwqi digital archives.[17]

I will shortly return to the discussion of the studio wedding photograph. Here, I want to note that the change in wedding outfits and the ceremonial studio wedding photographs did not happen in any neat temporal order, as the couple in figure 2.12 (identities unknown) wear traditional wedding outfits in a studio photograph. Furthermore, the outfits shown here are clearly from elite, mostly urban, families. As Sohelia Shahshahani has noted, "Silk and velvet were very pricey, and were considered suitable . . . for brides. The bride's skirt was densely pleated, using 10–15 meters of fabric. . . . Brides wore pantaloons under the short skirt."[18]

The shift to the white wedding gown of the bride and the tuxedo of the groom made the bride and the groom a different couple from their parents. The conjugal couple was now sartorially distinct from the rest of their families within the scene of marital celebration. Previously, brides and grooms wore fancier clothes, but generally not clothes uniquely marked as wedding clothes or necessarily and uniquely distinct from those of the guests.

In Iran, in some aristocratic families, the white European-style wedding dress made its entry by the second decade of the twentieth century. 'Ayn al-Saltaneh (1872–1945), in his memoirs, notes on 5 October 1917 the novelty of two wedding dresses that had been tailored like those in Europe (Farangistan), "white, with a long train on the back that has to be carried by the bride's maids."[19]

The change was uneven and partial, often class-specific. In Mihrmah Farmanfarmayan's household, the wedding gown of Ma'sumeh — the daughter of Kal Hadi, the old gardener of their Shimiran garden — was pink silk with a white veil to cover her face. This was around 1925. A decade and a class apart, Mihrmah's own 1935 wedding gown was a full white gown with a long, flowing train (fig. 2.13).[20] Even into the 1940s, at times some aspects of the wedding clothes would change, but not others: for instance, adding a white lace veil to a colorful dress, as in the studio photograph shown in figure 2.14.

The change slowly began to inform urban culture more broadly. Yet it isn't clear that, for early generations, the wedding outfits were necessarily affectively significant. For my mother, Fari, and her older sister, 'Iffat, the wedding dress as such was not uniquely and individually emotionally invested. From a relatively lower middling economic bracket, it made no sense to get a new dress for Fari. For her wedding, she wore the same dress that 'Iffat had worn over a year earlier. The significant event was to be dressed in one and take a studio photograph in it. Fari and 'Iffat had identical studio wedding photographs (figs. 2.15–2.16).

From the early 1930s, for many middle-class urban couples, going to a professional studio in wedding clothes and staging "conjugal coupledom" in

FIGURE 2.8. Men's wedding outfit, early nineteenth century. Source: http://www.qajarwomen.org/en/items/1139A184.html.

FIGURE 2.9. Turan Qahrimani's wedding dress. Source: http://www.qajarwomen.org/en/items/1391A44.html.

FIGURE 2.10. A wedding skirt with velvet embroidery, a folded segment of skirt for Shams al-Muluk Jahanbani's wedding. Source: http://www.qajarwomen.org/en /items/42a040.html.

front of the photographic lens became part of the ceremony, as Fari's remembrance of her wedding day indicates. In her memoir, Fari describes her wedding in great detail, with much evident pleasure, as a very happy event:

> My wedding took place with simplicity, as I had wanted. . . . We were deeply happy. . . . After 'aqd [the formal wedding contract], everyone gathered in the big guest talar and we had tea and sweets; then the guests left. . . . In the evening, we went to a photographic studio and took a very nice picture in [my] white wedding dress and my husband's black outfit. It is a nice memory piece. We then went to the house of my elder brother who had become like a father to me and celebrated with some of 'Abbas's friends and my family and friends. We laughed and danced all night and had dinner.

The nonstudio wedding photographs were often of familial groups; at times the bride and the groom would be photographed with a most important patriarch, as in a photograph of Bihjat al-Muluk Mu'izzi and 'Abd

FIGURE 2.11. Naqdah wedding dress, made of tulle embroidered with gold and silver thread. Source: Center for Iranian Jewish Oral History. http://www .qajarwomen.org/en /items/1025A209.html.

FIGURE 2.12. Unknown photographer, couple in studio, date unknown, albumen print, University Library, Tehran. Source: Carmen Pérez González, *Local Portraiture*, 311. Used with permission of the author.

مـهـرمـاه فـرمانفرماییان، روز عـقدکنان در روی پلههای سـالن بیرونی
فرمانفرما برداشته شده است.

آبان‌ماه ۱۳۱۴

FIGURE 2.13. Mihrmah
Farmanfarmayan's wedding dress.
Source: Farmanfarmayan,
Zir-i nigah-i pidar, 330.

FIGURE 2.14. Raf'at al-Muluk
Qahiri and Yusif Jalili Tehrani.
Source: http://www.qajar
women.org/en/items/1274A23
.html.

FIGURE 2.15. Fari and 'Abbas's wedding photograph, 14 January 1942. Source: Family album.

FIGURE 2.16. 'Iffat and 'Isa's wedding photograph, 1 August 1940. Source: Family album.

FIGURE 2.17. Bihjat al-Muluk Muʻizzi and ʻAbd Allah Ashraf's wedding photograph. Source: http://www.qajarwomen.org/en/items/1138A17.html.

Allah Ashraf with the bride's uncle (fig. 2.17). As Kenneth Cuno has argued, "Regardless of whether they lived in a joint or conjugal family household, couples who posed for intimate photos . . . presented themselves as bourgeois conjugal families."[21] These photographs, framing the couple in their distinct clothes, not only reflected the process of idealization of the conjugal couple, but also contributed to its power incessantly: these photographs were framed and displayed in the home in prominent places, on walls, on cupboards and bookshelves, or on top of pianos in more prosperous homes.[22] Their ubiquitous visual presence—one saw them every day, one saw them in most urban middle-class homes—contributed to the crafting of its normative idealness. The emergence of the studio wedding photograph, along with the visual distinction of the bride and the groom displayed by their outfits, contributed to the self-evidence of conjugality of the family.

Family Photographs

The changes in familial concepts and practices of everyday life coincided with the arrival of photography in the Middle East. Photography came to some of the urban centers of the Ottoman domains and to Qajar Iran shortly after its invention in 1841.[23] Both the camera and the family photograph were among those objects of everyday life that generatively contributed to the changes in concepts and practices that they were to record and archive. Photographs, in particular family photographs, are "evocative objects," to use Sherry Turkle's idea, "underscoring the inseparability of thought and feeling in our relationship to things. We think with the objects we love; we love the objects we think with."[24] At times, they render, as G. Arunima has put it, "certain modern familial moments (for example, birthdays or weddings) into events."[25]

Historians and cultural analysts have done vastly different things with family photographs and albums. For example, Annette Kuhn, by looking at photographs from her own childhood—some alone, one with her mother when Kuhn was four months of age (two copies, hers, and another with her mother's notes on the verso), one at the time of Queen Elizabeth II's coronation—and other photographs and film stills, Kuhn narrates stories of her relationships to her mother and her father, her mother's relationship with her father, and others.[26] Her stories and her readings of the photographs are deeply informed by psychoanalytic approaches to memory and ways of seeing.

I take a different approach, more inspired by material object historians, such as Laurel Ulrich and Janet Hoskins.[27] I take up the materiality of the photograph and its circulation, and include photographs and family albums among those "domestic objects—ordinary household possessions that might be given an extraordinary significance by becoming entangled in the events of a person's life and used as a vehicle for a sense of selfhood," as Hoskins points out, perhaps a more appropriate approach toward biographical objects "in a society that has not been 'psychologized' in a confessional tradition."[28]

Family photographs and albums come to life through oral tales about them or other stories they evoke, which bring out layers of meaning out of the flat surface of the photograph.[29] In a way, similar to Sharon Marcus's "just reading," I wonder if we have enacted an injustice to the reading of family photographs by at times single-mindedly trying to excavate through them layers of psychoanalytical insight for family relations, between mother and daughter, father and daughter, oedipal and pre-oedipal, and so on.[30] What if, instead of engaging in reading practices that attempt to "pierce through the photograph's flat surface," we read superficially, stayed on the surface, and, instead of employing psychoanalytically informed reading practices, tuned into oral stories about the photograph to hear multiple viewpoints?[31]

This kind of reading photographs becomes possible with increased access to multigenre archives. My work, for example, has been enabled by the WWQI digital archive and website. I have worked on this archive since 2009, along with a large group of scholars, editors, photographers, and project managers. We visit families to photograph and digitize their relevant documents, photographs, and objects of daily life. Within that context, we have heard numerous stories of lives. A photograph brings out a memory, and an object becomes the occasion for recalling a relative's wedding. Seeing photographs together with hearing family stories thus informs my understanding of what family photographs and albums have done for our concepts and practices of the family.

Like the change in the wedding outfits, and studio photographs, as I discussed in the previous sections, family photographs became increasingly couple-centered and marked conjugalization of the family. Malek Alloula, in a chapter titled "Couple," discusses the couple as a misreading of the European camera, "an aberration, a historical error, an unthinkable possibility in Algerian society."[32] But by the early decades of the twentieth century, the couple picture had become a "nativized" performance of marriages in many Middle Eastern countries, including Egypt, Iran, and Turkey, itself an indication of conjugalization of the ideal family. Numerous "husband and wife" photographs on the WWQI website attest to the performance of conjugality as family.[33] I include a few here as an invitation for readers to browse the collection (figs. 2.18–2.20). Some photographs, at times printed as postcards, were sent or given to other kin and friends (fig. 2.21), thus further contributing to the crafting of the conjugal couple-as-family through circulation among a larger social network.

But the conjugal photograph was not the only scene of photographic familiality. Taking occasional family photographs, often at particular celebratory moments when the whole family got together, would produce other performances of the familial.[34] These presentations were not necessarily conjugally centered; generally, they marked the sense of the familial formed around the most senior members of the group. The latter could be the most

FIGURE 2.18. Rahil and
David Aminuf. Source:
http://www.qajarwomen
.org/en/items/1025A125
.html.

FIGURE 2.19. Heripsima
and her husband. Source:
http://www.qajarwomen
.org/en/items/1144A91
.html.

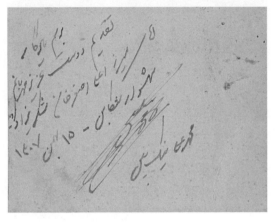

FIGURES 2.20 and 2.21.
Muhammad ʿAli Nik Bin
and his wife. On the back
the photo is dedicated to
a friend of Mr. Nik Bin's.
Source: http://www
.qajarwomen.org/en
/items/14146A21.html.

senior conjugal couple, or other familial elders, especially in households that
continued to live as generationally combined ones, in some cities well into
the middle decades of the twentieth century.

Family photographs and albums worked as important cultural objects, as
one of the technologies that generated who counted as kin. Different inclusions and exclusions continue to this day, indicating that practices, despite
the ideational power of the concept of the conjugal couple as family, are var-
ied in important ways. Indeed, photography has been used as well to generate
a sense of the familial that at times worked against its conjugalization. From
the photographs of one family, the Mallahs and Vaziris (figs. 2.22–2.26),
several indicate a purposeful, insistent inclusion of children from different

FIGURE 2.22. Mallah family. Source: http://www.qajarwomen.org/en/items/
14129A17.html.

wives, for example, at times using collages to clearly and decidedly include
persons as family. In the collage reproduced as figure 2.22, conjugal centeredness is fully on display. At the same time, children and grandchildren from
other marriages have been folded into the family.

The writing at the center of the collage reads "the Mallah Family." The
conjugal couple—Khadijeh Afzal Vaziri (1890–1980) and her husband,
Aqa Buzurg Mallah (1884–1964)—constitute the nodal point of the collage, or what the eye is captured by on first glance. Khanum Afzal was Aqa
Buzurg's second wife. Included here are, from top left, counterclockwise: Zu-
bayadeh Mallah (the daughter of Aqa Buzurg Mallah from his first wife),
Mahlaqa Mallah (1917–), Amir Hushang Mallah (1919–), Husayn'ali Mallah
(1921–1992), Nusrat Allah Changizi, Behrouz Bayat (son of Mahlaqa Mallah
and her first husband, Muhammad Zaman Bayat), Guli Mallah (daughter
of Nusrat Zaman, Aqa Buzurg's third wife—a co-wife with Khadijeh Khanum), Khusraw Mallah (1927–), and Mihrangiz Mallah (1923–2013).

Significantly, in her portrait Khanum Afzal is shown at a table, in the
gesture of writing. Like her mother, Bibi Khanum Astarabadi, and her sister

FIGURE 2.23. Khanum Afzal in outer garment and headcover for going to work. Source: http://www.qajarwomen.org/en/items/14129A57.html.

FIGURE 2.24. Khanum Afzal tutoring her children, circa 1929. Source: http://www.qajarwomen.org/fa/items/14129A50.html.

FIGURE 2.25. Mallah family, circa 1960. Source: http://www.qajarwomen.org/en/items/14129A36.html.

FIGURE 2.26. Mallah family, circa 1930. Source: http://www.qajarwomen.org/en/items/14129A53.html.

Maulud A'lam al-Saltaneh, Khanum Afzal was among the early pioneers of women's education and wrote in the press about women's rights.[35] Her children, in particular her two daughters, Mahlaqa and Mihrangiz, were proud of their mother's achievements. In this central photograph, she is also wearing the outer garment that she had designed to show that women could go to work in decent clothes without needing to wear the traditional chador and face cover (fig. 2.23). Furthermore, the table behind which she is positioned is the same one at which she used to tutor her two daughters (fig. 2.24). The collage, thus, not only insistently constructs an expansive sense of the conjugally centered Mallah family. It also insistently emphasizes the modernness of the family and the pride of the daughters in their mother as a modern woman, writer, and educator.

Photographs, just like texts, do not have a singular intrinsic meaning. Reading this collage as the Mallahs' purposeful inclusion of siblings from multiple wives as family is informed by seeing many other family photographs they have cherished and the stories they have told about persons and photographs. The repeated visualization of the generationally expansive and genealogically inclusive Mallah family, along with conjugal photographs or conjugally centered photographs, demonstrates the many complex ways that families in real life made up their family-ness (figs. 2.25–2.26). As Mahlaqa Mallah once put it in a nutshell, "We lived tribally [*ilyati*]; people became integrated into the Mallah family from all kinds of directions."[36]

Despite the twentieth-century ideational near dominance of love-based (monogamous) marriage and the conjugally centered family, people have continued to live vastly complex familial lives. Conjugalization has remained an unfinished and unfinishable project. It demanded a rearranging of one's attachments and loyalties within the familial network, putting the loyalty between the conjugal couple above those between parents and child, among siblings, with aunts and cousins, and even with friends. This was neither a smooth nor achieved process once and for all. Wives continued to travel a great deal with sisters and female friends, rather than with their husbands. They continued to keep close intimate ties to sisters and female friends, at times to the exclusion of their husbands from these intimacies.[37]

3. Meanings of Marriage
Forming a Family or Providing Sexual Pleasure

The changes in familial practices were not simply an effect of the emerging ideational dominance of love-based marriage and the conjugally centered couple as a family. These changes were intimately connected with changes in what marriage was meant for in the first place.

Modern reconfigurations of the meaning of forming a family worked with classical ethics of marriage. In classical Islamic books of ethics, the domains of love, friendship, taking (sexual) pleasure, and acquiring a wife were distinct.[1] All were considered as necessary parts of a perfect man's life; each had its own purpose, reason, and manners of conduct. When it came to "getting a wife," these books emphasized that the purpose of marriage was not satisfaction of sexual desire (tamattu'), for which, they suggested, there were other venues. The prime purpose of "getting a wife," instead, was ta'ahhul, or forming a household and begetting children.[2] This, of course, did not exclude sexual pleasure for husband *and* wife, as the female orgasm was thought to be necessary for conception. But, it was argued, God created sexual desire in men in order for them to engage in sexual intercourse in order to guarantee procreation. Marriage was also recommended to ensure a man's piety—to seek sexual satisfaction licitly, even when aroused by women who were not one's wife or by male adolescents.

For women, ta'ahhul and tamattu' were presumed to be always coincidental; legally and in terms of social acceptance, there could be no licit practice of sexual pleasure for women outside marriage. Not so for men, who practiced the distinction licitly: not only could they take several wives, but they could engage as well in various other practices, including concubinage in the Ottoman domains and sigheh marriages in Qajar Iran.

A dictionary definition of *ahl* might include family, relatives, folks, kin, kinfolk, more specifically a wife, and, somewhat distinctly, people, members, followers, and adherents.[3] Thus, ta'ahhul bears the meaning of forming a family through getting a wife. Yet the second group of ahl's meanings bears on this conception as well. When speaking of *ahl-i manzil*, it connotes people/members of the house (*manzil*, abode).

The expression "ahl-i manzil" reflects and generates the household-centeredness of what we generally refer to as "family" in English. "People of the house" included one's wife (wives) and children (and possibly parents and siblings), but also nonblood or marriage-related kinfolk, including (depending on one's social status) servants, cooks, wet nurses, tutors, horsemen, and managers. In other words, ta'ahhul had at its core the forming of a household. In this sense, it bears resemblance to a similar concept, "household-family," as argued by Naomi Tadmor for seventeenth- and eighteenth-century England.[4] "'Family' in their language could mean a household, including its diverse dependents such as servants, apprentices and co-resident relatives. Accordingly, [Samuel] Johnson defined 'family' as 'those who live in the same house.' . . . To be sure, there was a concept of 'family' in seventeenth- and eighteenth-century England emanating from relationships of blood and marriage. But . . . there was also a related yet different, and highly significant, concept of the family emanating from relationships of co-residence and authority."[5]

The household-forming aim of marriage also defined who would constitute the right woman for ta'ahhul, as distinct from a woman for tamattu'. Similarly, the appropriate sentiment for each relation differed: generally, muhibbat (affection), not 'ishq (love), was the sentiment to be cultivated between a husband and wife. This continued to inform the modern reconceptualization of marriage. As we saw in chapter 1, even in modern novels, 'ishq was largely depicted as a family-destroying passion rather than a family-forming affect. Ta'ahhul was perceived under siege by the kind of love that the novels were seen to have popularized, even as much fiction critiqued the family-destroying force of passionate love.

The household-centeredness of marriages and the meaning of family also undergird some of the common intrafamilial practices of marriage that aimed to hold the household together (beyond the usual understanding of these practices as economically driven), such as marrying one's deceased husband's brother, or marrying one's deceased wife's sister. Marriages were, after all, between households and not between individual persons. Thus, the emphasis on elder advice and selection (rather than youthful choice that could be as erratic as sexual passion itself) and on kufu — social class and cultural parity and compatibility.

With the emerging dominance of love/affection-based marriage as the ideal of family formation, young women's expectation of how they would marry perhaps changed even more drastically than those of young men. Men, after all, already had freer socializing options and, as many women observed, they also held the prerogative over divorce, should a family-arranged marriage not work out. Young women, especially those educated in the modern schools for girls and perhaps already aspiring to a career, such as my mother, Fari, her sisters, and work colleagues, began to display more open modes of marriage resistance. Getting rid of unwanted suitors, as we saw in chapter 1, seemed to become a generational practice. It indicates an emergent expectation about the selection of your future mate. Even if one did not necessarily expect to fall in love madly with one's future spouse, it was expected that one would at least get to know the person and be happy with a parentally suggested mate.

In Iran, into the twentieth century, mut'a/sigheh marriage continued to be practiced for seeking sexual pleasure licitly but not familially. Unlike a permanent *nikah*, its aim was not to beget children, even though if any children were born in a mut'a marriage they would have the same legal and inheritance status as those born to permanent wives. At times, children born of a mut'a wife would make the marriage more long-lasting, if not legally permanent. It is here that the biggest shift in familial concepts and practices occurred as conjugally centered, love-informed, and partner-selected marriage acquired its desirability.

Contracting a mut'a marriage increasingly became a sign of undesirable, culturally conservative backwardness. For men from a segment of the urban upper classes the practice was replaced by taking a maîtresse; even flaunting such an illicit practice in public socializing acquired at times dubious but nonetheless circulating recognition. Taking a maîtresse became associated with becoming Europeanized, *farangi-ma'abi*. For critics, what had been viewed as largely practices of courtiers and aristocrats, and at sociopolitically volatile times read as a sign of corruption, now was alarmingly spreading like a disease (and indeed was seen to spread venereal diseases as well) to larger layers of urban men — a sign of Europeanized moral corruption.

To have a sigheh wife or to take a maîtresse became a cultural distinction: Shaykh 'Abbas Nadim, about whose marriages we will learn more later in this chapter, took as his third concurrent wife a sigheh. For modern, upper-class men, taking a sigheh, and at times bigamy, became a cultural practice of conservative Muslim backwardness. In spring 1945, Zohreh, the young wife

of 'Ali Mahmud (a European-educated successful architect), suffered a serious injury that rendered her paraplegic and led to her early death several
years later. During these years, Zohreh was tortured by the fear that her husband 'Ali might take another wife. 'Ali would not entertain that option, even
though he apparently, according to what he told their son, had many affairs.
'Ali repeatedly emphasized that he had no plans to marry another woman.
Only after Zohreh's death did he marry, and it was not one of his maîtresses
but a woman from the larger familial network. His story also indicates how
modern sensibilities had begun to work against bigamy even under conditions that in earlier times and among more tradition-minded families would
have been considered perfectly understandable for a man to take a second
wife, and indeed it may have been encouraged by the first wife herself.

As 'Ali Mahmud's story indicates, women kept as maîtresses by modern,
upper-class men were seen not as appropriate for a family-forming marriage,
yet they were suited and in demand for extramarital sexual pleasure and as appropriate social partners to take to the emerging clubs and social functions —
eminently nonfamilial spaces in the early decades of the twentieth century.
These spaces were desirous of the presence of women to dance with, laugh
with, and have fun with — namely, the emergent modern practices of pleasure, or tamattu'.

This also meant that there was an emerging layer of women — some Europeans, some non-Muslims, but also some from Muslim households — who
became integrated into this socializing culture. These included some high
aristocratic women, who became marked as public women, such as Taj al-
Saltaneh, Nasir al-Din Shah's daughter. Her first marriage, arranged in 1893
by her father, ended in divorce in late 1907. Subsequently, she married twice
more (in 1908 and 1909); neither marriage lasted very long. In subsequent
years, she became part of the more openly heterosocializing urban, upper-
class culture. Along with a number of courtly women, she was rumored to
have sexual relations with men. She was considered a royal whore.[6]

One possibly fictitious diary is rather appreciative of the practices of the
time. Among the papers of my father, 'Abbas, was a curious booklet (fig. 3.1).
Measuring nineteen centimeters by twelve centimeters, seventy pages of the
notebook had the writings of a person, self-named 'Ali Akbar Sa'i.[7] Containing exquisite handwriting, the booklet certainly could not have been penned
by 'Abbas, who had terrible handwriting; it was a presumably fictional piece
of writing.[8]

FIGURE 3.1. A notebook among 'Abbas's papers. Source: Author's holdings.

After a paragraph of explaining his reasons for writing (as a historically useful note and for personal improvement), he writes that two people will be at the center of these notes, himself and his beloved, whom he only refers to as F-Y and gives the nickname Venus. The diary is totally focused on a three-year relationship the narrator had developed with a "public" woman living in his neighborhood, Amiriyeh. He writes solely on daily matters related to this relationship; he had met F-Y six months prior to when he begins to write these notes.

The notebook prose has a fictional feel to it. In a few places, where the writer addresses the reader, it seems that it was assumed that it would have a readership, rather than kept as a private diary; however, this kind of direct address appears in many of the diaries of the period. Reading it as fiction or fact, the notebook indicates that practices of men's street socializing with women, with the aim of possible sexual liaisons, had emerged as a practice worthy of recording. The author's loving infatuation with Venus is recorded on page after page; each day's reporting is structured around whether he succeeded in seeing her, meeting up with her, whether she paid attention to him, what he purchased from Laleh-zar shops for her, her demands on him, and finally a night spent with her. He writes over two and a half pages about details of the night, followed by another two pages in the following days reflecting on the night, at times regretting that it finally happened after three years, and whether the sadness that has gripped him since was worth the union. Some three weeks later, during which he writes very briefly, at times only one line, the diary ends. That the entries stop shortly after the description of the one night he spends at Venus's house gives the larger meaning of the diary and the relationship as one in the category of a pleasure relationship (tamattu'). It is also important to note that his recording of these daily events is always set within and echoes the culture of men hanging out on the streets with friends regularly. Generally, none of the street interactions the author records are solo activities. They are street, social practices that groups of young men engaged in together. The narrator is presumably from an urban, elite family, does not seem to need to earn a living, and refers to the only other female character (appearing three times) as *hazrat-i 'illiyeh* (a highly respectful way of referring to a woman, who could be either his wife or possibly his mother but it is not clear).

The social reception toward this new practice of maîtresse keeping was rather ambivalent, even among the upper middle classes, and within gossip circulation. 'Ali Mahmud's son recalled his father's liaisons with bitterness and anger, as something that hurt his mother, Zohreh, and himself and had created many family quarrels. He recalled, with equal disapproval, his uncle who had either taken a second permanent wife or a sigheh, causing his wife much misery. Kaukab Khanum, whom we met in chapter 1, in the context of commenting on her husband's prior marriage as a sigheh marriage, indicated that other men in the family were not much better; her uncle was known to have one wife but several maîtresses.

At times, even a long-lasting affectionate bond between a woman and a man would be broken at the time of the man's marriage due to familial considerations. Publicly socializing women were not deemed appropriate for marriage. Occasionally, however, a woman who socialized in the new milieu did marry her male partner; such was the case with Tatiyana Markariyan, the second wife of 'Abd al-Husayn Taymurtash. This particular marriage also has the marking of a transition period in which one may have married traditionally and nontraditionally. Some Iranian men had returned from their years in

Europe with European wives. This had become a topic of much social debate and critique, including by women's rights activists such as Sadiqeh Dawla-tabadi.[9] Taymurtash's two wives would fit in a different way in this bifurca-tion. For a respectable woman from a well-known, respected urban family, such as Surur al-Saltaneh, mixing in these public venues of clubs and garden parties was probably not yet appropriate: after all, that is what had gained a woman like Taj al-Saltaneh the prostitute reputation. Taymurtash reportedly attended such parties with Tatiyana.[10] Upon marriage to Taymurtash, Tati-yana was set up in a different house and that is where receptions for ambas-sadors and other Europeans were held, "feasts and passing a pleasurable time ['aysh] were held in that house."[11]

Who got to be taken into the familial household, and who could not or would not be in, signals what family meant. A maîtresse could never be taken into the familial (conjugal) household or be considered as family under any circumstance. A second permanent wife could be taken into a shared house-hold or set up in another residence, but a sigheh wife was usually not taken into a familial residence. Even in cases where contracting a sigheh wife was suggested by the permanent wife, the sigheh wives lived in the shadow of the familial household.

In some families, when a son turned fifteen (or was seen to have reached puberty/sexual maturity, *bulugh*), parents would contract a sigheh wife for him to ensure that his sexual urges would find a licit aim.[12] These contracts were considered truly temporary and "premarital"; once the son was in a po-sition to settle into a family-forming marriage, they were considered unneces-sary. Within large households, female members of the serving/servant crew would at times act, willingly or not, as "sexual initiators" for adolescent sons. In more observant families, such initiating practice would be sanctioned by a sigheh contract, either openly or as a secret that everyone knew about. Par-ents hoped that providing the possibility of licit sexual mates would keep their sons under familial control and safe from what was called *jindeh-bazi* (becom-ing a regular customer of prostitutes). Mushfiq Kazimi writes about how on the wedding night of his uncle, there were two women in the household who seemed sad. One was a woman who had been for a while the uncle's *jameh-dar*, the servant in charge of taking care of and arranging his clothes. "Secretly [*dar khafa*], she was also his sigheh. With the wedding, she would now lose her status; ... she was sitting in semi-darkness, with a sad face, on the stair behind where the festivities were going on. ... The second person was a woman, who also had a relationship with my uncle and everyone knew about it; her socializing with the guests was deemed inappropriate. . . . Finally, some of the guests insisted and she agreed to dance to the music of entertainers."[13]

Sigheh marriages could at times form families, as was the case with 'Ayn al-Saltaneh's sigheh marriages. 'Ayn al-Saltaneh, a nephew of Nasir al-Din Shah, had been married at the age of seventeen to his first permanent wife, Rubabeh Khanum (Galin Khanum). When no child was born from this marriage, in 1892, he took a second wife, Kaukab Dargahi, whose father was a gatekeeper (*darban*) of Nasir al-Din Shah's andaruni.[14] This marriage is recorded as a time-limited marriage, that is, mut'a, but the length of the marriage is not specified in the contract. This would make the marriage equivalent to a permanent marriage, but, in his memoirs, he specifically calls this marriage a mut'a marriage, possibly because of Kaukab Dargahi's inferior social status. Over the years, he had five daughters from Kaukab Khanum—Nuzhat al-Muluk, Qamar al-Dawleh, 'Ayn al-Muluk, Malakeh, and Raushanak; their only son died at the age of ten months. Galin Khanum died from cholera on 9 July 1904. This left 'Ayn al-Saltaneh with no class-appropriate wife. He was next married to Shazdeh Baygum Khanum (Mufarrah al-Dawleh) on 30 July 1905. This was not a happy match from the start. As a royal woman, she had insisted that 'Ayn al-Saltaneh should divorce Kaukab first; but Kaukab had been yet again pregnant at the time and 'Ayn al-Saltaneh was clearly fond of her and reluctant to let go of the wife who had given him children — repeatedly in his memoirs he refers to her as "mother of my children." After a short period, Mufarrah al-Dawleh lived separately; she died on 25 March 1913. Next, he married another woman from the royalty, Mihrmah Khanum. Shortly after this marriage, he went for a long period to manage his father's estates in the Alamut area. Mihrmah Khanum refused to join him and eventually asked for and received her divorce. While in Alamut, after failing to persuade his new wife to join him, he eventually married, on 14 July 1911, a local woman, Zaynab, also as a time-limited, mut'a marriage, though set for ninety-nine years (effectively for life).[15] He had three sons from this marriage, 'Abbas, Mas'ud, and Bahman. Zaynab indeed remained his wife for life; he did not marry another woman. Already, in an entry written on 21 November 1912, he expressed his deep attachment to her: "I am apprehensive about writing of Zaynab's good qualities [*khubi* and *niku'i*]. . . . [S]he is a rural woman but far more intelligent than any urban woman, far more hard-working, far more accomplished in arts and crafts, with a serene temperament, with no troublesome brouhaha; I have come to develop affection and love for her."[16] Throughout his voluminous memoirs, he repeatedly writes about her qualities and his deep admiration for and attachment to her. His father, 'Izz al-Dawleh (who had a reputation for managing his six sigheh wives peaceably and after the death of his permanent wife did not take another permanent wife), was also fond of Zaynab, and he advised his son to give up on trying to mend relations with Mihrmah Khanum: "She isn't suitable for you, to hell with what you have spent on her. Someone who has a wife like Zaynab doesn't need to go after women like that."[17] Later in life (in 1937), 'Ayn al-Saltaneh writes that he had wanted to change the marriage contract to a permanent one so that Zaynab would receive a proper share of inheritance. She had refused, as was the case with successful sigheh marriages, with the wife believing that the marriage had happened at an auspicious moment and changing the moment of the marriage contract might produce discord. He then put the new house he was purchasing in her name and transferred to her the ownership of all of the house's contents.[18]

It is possibly this sigheh's potential for family-forming unions that became completely erased from familial practices with the dominance of conjugally centered, love-focused, modern marriage. Not only did sigheh become marked as a legal veneer for prostitution, but also women who engaged in such contracts became marked as "bad women" or alternatively as socioeconomic victims.[19]

The post-1979 recuperation of sigheh marriages, in particular by Muslim-observant women who wished to engage in sexual relations but not necessarily commit themselves to a long-term, family-forming union, is perhaps the beginning of rethinking the possibilities of sigheh anew and in an off-modern mode.[20]

Managing a Husband's New Marriage

Finding out about one's husband's new marriage incited a range of responses and practices toward one's husband, the other wife, and, more significantly, the latter's children. My maternal grandmother (Fari's mother) took the news of her husband's second marriage in silence, a silent strike. She stopped doing any housework. It must have been mid-summer. There were trays of boiled, crushed tomatoes on the roof to make paste for the year. All went moldy and had to be discarded. Eventually the silent strike came to an end; she went on with her familial life and had six more children. Fari talked about her mother's silent strike several times: at times in the context of what marriages used to be like *then*; at times in praise of her mother's patience (saburi) in life.[21]

Shazdeh Muluk and Salar Fatih's marriage had started as a love marriage; indeed, it had been initially opposed by her family (because his family's social standing had been considered below theirs). When Salar Fatih was posted to Muhammareh (now Khurramshahr), he took another wife (Khadijeh Sultan, daughter of a local Arab dignitary). Visiting her husband with their children, Shazdeh Muluk had been visited by Khadijeh Sultan, who came to pay her respect, introduce herself, and indicate that she was pregnant. Shazdeh Muluk, determined that her husband's child deserved a class- and ethnic-appropriate upbringing, brought the new wife to Tehran with her. Khadijeh Sultan was much younger, and Shazdeh Muluk took her in almost as a daughter.

Beyond silence, brief domestic strikes, and putting up with things patiently, there were other styles of facing the arrival of another wife into one's marriage. When Halimeh Khanum's husband of many years, Asad Allah Khan, with whom she already had two daughters and two sons, brought home a young wife, Halimeh declared to her husband that from then on, they were like "brother and sister." The second marriage ended in divorce, but he married again, this time with 'Alamtaj Khanum. Halimeh continued to live in the same household with 'Alamtaj and her children, and she outlived her husband/brother by seven years (see fig. 3.2).

The declaration of becoming siblings marks a point at which the wife considers herself no longer in a licit sexual contract with her husband. They have become sexually forbidden to each other. Fakhr 'Uzma Arghun recalled the moment when she had been led by her nanny's daughter to the room, where her husband was said to be with another woman, as the moment that she and he had become forbidden to each other (*namahram*) because the trust between them had been shattered.[22] Similarly, according to family stories, the father of Fari's older sister's husband openly had several extramarital relationships. His wife had in later years abstained from having sexual relations with him: she would leave a pair of slippers outside her bedroom chamber, signaling that she was in, but refused to have him there.

The decision to stay in the same residential quarter with one's husband — from whom one now felt estranged — and possibly his new (often much younger) wife may have had multiple reasons. For one thing, wives became affectionately attached to their husbands of many years, even if the marriage had been an arranged one. By the time a new wife arrived, they often had children who perhaps mattered to them more than the husband. Despite losing the privilege of being the only wife, as the senior woman of the household, one may have continued to be in a powerful and respected position. Further-

FIGURE 3.2. Family photo. The two adult women: 'Alamtaj (*right*) and Halimeh (*left*). Source: Tajpour album.

more, living outside a familial space was possibly an undesirable option as well as a financially difficult one.

At times, women considered divorce more shameful than living within a bad marriage or with another wife. In her memoirs, Mihrmah Farmanfarmayan narrates the story of Khadijeh Sultan, one of the domestics in her father's household. Khadijeh Sultan and her paternal cousin had started a loving marriage, against his mother's wishes (whom Khadijeh Sultan holds responsible for the eventual failure of the marriage). Eventually, he divorces her and marries a much younger woman. At this point in the story, Mihrmah's nanny says that at least he paid her mahr and her father supported her.

Khadijeh Sultan says, "What did I want my mahr for, when I had to return to the corner of my father's house? What of it if he had kept me and married the second wife? People live with *havu* [a co-wife], don't they? Having a havu is less humiliating than being divorced."[23]

For women, initiating divorce depended critically on a supportive family. Even then, at times it cast a shadow of ill repute over the entire family. At times, people would be warned against "taking a wife" from, or marrying into, such families: "their women are prone to ask for divorce."[24]

One's family support and social status were particularly critical when children were involved in a divorce. When Fakhr 'Uzma Arghun was told of (and possibly witnessed) her husband's extramarital liaisons, she left her marital home, although she was in her third month of pregnancy. She took her belongings and, along with her nanny (Tayeh Khanum) and the latter's daughter, returned to her father's house. Even with her father's full support, it took her four years before she could get a divorce.[25]

This was a particularly painful moment in her life. As we saw in chapter 1, her marriage to 'Abbas Khalili had started like an enactment of a modern love-marriage script between a modern, young man and an educated, modern woman. Within two weeks, Khalili was arrested on the order of Riza Khan (soon to become Riza Shah) and sent to internal exile. He returned from this exile after two years, in part due to Fakhri's persistent lobbying of Riza Shah. Their relationship after this interregnum was no longer a loving relation, Fakhri recalled. During his exile, he wrote his famous novel, *Ruzgar-i siyah* (Dark days), about the terrible life of "disreputable" women. This novel had alarmed Fakhri; she wondered if the realism of the novel was experientially based.[26]

The recurrent visits of women to their house and the eventual possible witnessing of her husband during one such visit prompted Fakhri's departure from her marital home and pursuing a divorce. Yet later in life, when her second husband surreptitiously married a young woman (with the marriage ceremony held in their house garden, under a mid-Sha'ban festivity pretext), and she found out the actual occasion after several days, she locked her husband out of the house and subsequently did not reconcile with him even though they were never divorced.[27]

Open and Secret Marriages

Men seem to have practiced both open and surreptitious multiple marriages. Shaykh 'Abbas, my cousin Qamar's husband's father, practiced both. His first wife, Sareh Khatun, had been his brother's wife. After the latter's death, Shaykh 'Abbas married her (not uncommon). They had a son and a daughter. After Sareh Khatun's death, he married Sareh's sister, often referred to as Abji (sister) Khanum by the children and grandchildren. When Shaykh 'Abbas's son from his marriage to Sareh died in a typhoid epidemic at the age of twenty, he found it intolerable to stay in Saveh and moved to Tehran. But Abji Khanum was not willing to leave her familial network and declared that she would remain in Saveh with her young son Ahmad (Qamar's future husband). Shaykh 'Abbas made it clear that if she didn't accompany him, he would have to take another wife in Tehran. This was a price that Abji Khanum was willing to pay to remain among her own kin. In Tehran, Shaykh 'Abbas married Fatimeh (called Khanum jun by her children and grandchildren). They lived in a house near Maydan Shah (now Maydan Qiyam). As Ahmad grew up, Abji Khanum found it difficult to manage him on her own and joined her husband in Tehran. She moved into Khanum jun's house. The two wives were housed in two rooms, across the middle courtyard. As family stories are told, Abji Khanum was received well and kindly by Khanum jun and had expressed visible respect and gratitude toward Khanum jun all her life. Shaykh 'Abbas would spend time with each wife in their rooms. Abji Khanum had one more son, born in Tehran; she died many years before Shaykh 'Abbas (d. 1930 or 1931/1309 Sh.). By 1930, Khanum jun had five sons and a daughter. I had never met Abji Khanum, and integration of her children into Khanum jun's household was so seamless that I had no idea Khanum jun was not Ahmad's biological mother until I began to interview family members about familial histories.

After Shaykh 'Abbas's death, a woman, also named Fatimeh, with a son (Hasan) and a daughter ('Iffat) showed up at Khanum jun's house, claiming to have been married to Shaykh 'Abbas and to have two children with him. This was a surprise to the family. Ahmad, however, stepped forward and confirmed Fatimeh's claim: his father had contracted a sigheh marriage with her and this marriage had produced two children. After the marriage's time period elapsed, he had continued to support Fatimeh and her two children by sending them monthly allowances, which Ahmad had been in charge of taking to them. Thus, two more siblings were added to the existing seven sons and one daughter of the household.[28]

Why Shaykh 'Abbas, already an openly bigamous man, had opted to keep his third marriage hidden, no one knows. It could be that the Maydan Shah residence was already overcrowded with two wives and many children. It could be, given the financial burden of supporting two wives and many children, that he had decided to settle for the less costly route of a mut'a marriage, contracted for sexual pleasure. Yet he seems to have developed an affectionately meaningful relationship with Fatimeh in order to stay in that marriage, generating two children. Perhaps, by the time of his marriage to Fatimeh, sigheh had already acquired its modern derogatory load, which prevented him from disclosing the marriage to his wives. Indeed, if the marriage had not produced children, Fatimeh may have disappeared from his life and Khanum jun would have never found out. Alternatively, it is possible that for men such as Shaykh 'Abbas, mut'a contracts offered a clear way of defining their familial marriage contracts (permanent 'aqd), distinct from their equally licit yet nonfamilial (nonpermanent) contracts for sexual pleasure. Even if children were born into the latter circumstance, recognized and supported as Shaykh 'Abbas did to his death, it could still not generate a familial domain, even as families expected such recognition for a sigheh wife's children.

The growing cultural gap between men like Shaykh 'Abbas and men who engaged in illicit sexual relations for pleasure had become the subject of much social critique, in particular in didactic novellas and novels of the early decades of the twentieth century. The best known of these were *Tihran-i makhauf* and *Ruzgar-i siyah*. The former discussed polygynous practices, and monogamy, or at least legal fidelity, was mentioned in the latter. Rather the difference resided in whether polygynous, nonfamilial sexual relations were engaged in licitly or illicitly. The nonlicit, extramarital sexual liaisons were viewed as largely practices of the Court and the courtiers and unconscionable men. At volatile times, they were read as signs of political corruption. Quite possibly, in the eyes of urban middle-class women, the difference between licit (sigheh) and illicit (taking a maîtresse) sexual relationships of their husbands ceased to be meaningful. Sigheh became viewed and experienced by many as prostitution.

Naming another wife as sigheh, whether factually accurate or not, in many women's narratives worked as a way of lowering the status of one's husband's other wife. The lowering weight of such narratives, contemporaneously or as told by later generations, would often be amplified by suggesting, again whether factually accurate or not, that the other woman was a domestic servant: only a lower-class woman would engage in sigheh, would prostitute herself, so the narrative went. One's husband's engagement in the practice would correspondingly be justified by temporal or spatial necessities. Recall Kaukab's story about her husband's first wife, "a house servant in a temporary marriage." His contracting of this marriage had been explained by the temporality of a young male adult not ready for settling down into a permanent marriage yet still interested in a licit sexual relationship. Shazdeh Muluk's husband's marriage to Khadijeh Sultan was also described as a sigheh justified by his being away from his family in Tehran, not to mention the local political alliance it may have facilitated.

Kaukab's grandmother, Zaynab Baygum, had been married to Haj Mahmud Mu'tamad al-Sultan. They had a daughter and a son. But the son died at the age of seven. With Zaynab Baygum's blessing, as the story is told, he contracted a sigheh marriage with Sakineh, one of their house servants. A son and a daughter ensued from this marriage; they became fully integrated into the household. Unbeknownst to Zaynab Baygum, Haj Mahmud contracted yet another sigheh wife. Another daughter, Nigar, was born from this marriage, but this time Zaynab Baygum refused to accept Nigar into her household. Nigar and her mother remained outsiders. Nigar's mother, a sigheh wife, was marginalized at the edges of the familial core, and no one remembers her name. This pattern of a wife's blessing, or at times even initiating, a marriage — usually a sigheh marriage — for her husband helped the wife to control her husband's polygynous desires and ensure her own privileged position as a permanent wife and the senior woman of the household. Zaynab Baygum here was the deciding person over which of her husband's children from subsequent marriages became family and which remained in the familial shadow.

Generational Changes in Family Practices

The complex shape of the Vaziri-Mallah familial network further conveys the differing and changing familial practices through three recent generations (see fig. 3.3). There is much investment in the narrative of the Vaziris and the Mallahs as modernist pioneers in several fields. Bibi Khanum Astarabadi was a pioneer of women's education, and her son 'Alinaqi Vaziri was the father of modern Iranian music. Another son, Hasan'ali Vaziri (a student of Kamal al-Mulk), was a modern painter, and in the next generation there

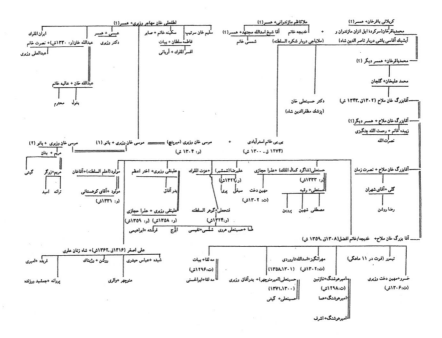

FIGURE 3.3. Genealogy of Vaziri/Mallah family. Source: Author's drawing.

is Mahlaqa Mallah, a pioneer of the environmental movement in Iran. This narrative has at times generated a tendency to erase what a writer has found to be incongruities between their life practices and their pioneering modernity. Yet, as we will see, Bibi Khanum's pursuit of keeping her school for girls open in her residence and arranging for a sigheh marriage for her husband are not incoherent actions that need tidying up. As a matter of fact, the former was enabled by the latter.

Neither were such practices of life experienced as incoherent or conflicting in the auto-narratives of Bibi Khanum and that of her daughter Afzal Khanum (Vaziri). In Bibi Khanum's autobiographical segment in *Ma'ayib al-rijal* (Vices of men), she has no qualms describing her own thoughts of getting another wife/domestic servant for her husband:

> I was mired in calamities for nine years, and gave birth to six children, four sons and two daughters. Because I had no milk, I needed a wet nurse, but I didn't have the means to hire one. I also needed a domestic who could stay in the house as a servant. Out of desperation, I finally thought of bringing a virgin maiden, whom I would let my husband

take instead of me. I thought this was an impossible delusion. . . . But thoughts did not leave me . . . until I reached the conclusion that nothing bad could come of seeking a wife for my husband. I would be the lady of the house and she would be a paid servant. I would then leave worries aside and ingratiate myself with my husband.[29]

Her plan eventually took shape; an elderly woman visited her one day, introducing "a childless widower" looking for a family to serve. The young woman, Hajieh Nisa', twenty years of age, had been brought to Tehran from Rasht, by another woman in whose house she had worked. Now, she was unhappy there and was seeking a new employer. From the start, Bibi Khanum marks the woman as morally suspect, not simply by referring to her city of origin as Rasht—a city that Tehranis had considered to have women who were loose and men not zealous enough to control their women—but also by telling us that she did not veil in front of male strangers.[30] Nevertheless, Bibi Khanum hires her and soon notices that Hajieh Nisa' is often anxious and fearful. She is apparently fearful that her previous employer might find her. They change her name to Banu, but she is found out anyway. Her former employer claims, "She is my son's sigheh. I have paid four hundred tumans to bring her here from Rasht." But Banu denies it and eventually her former employer gives up on her claim and leaves. Already suspicious and wary of Banu, Bibi Khanum "was nevertheless kind to her and gave her everything she wanted, including clothing, chador, jewelry, and money. In three months, I paid her more than I had promised. On occasions and in passing, I hinted at the issue of a sigheh with my husband."[31]

However, Bibi Khanum's husband's eventual contracting of Banu as a sigheh wife was unacceptable to Bibi Khanum because he had married Banu in her absence and without her knowledge—when she was spending a few days at the Court during Nauruz and Ramadan festivities. Moreover, the new marriage began to threaten her own marriage; it had happened out of her control and at her expense.[32]

Upon returning to her house after the Court festivities, she finds her husband quarrelsome and they get into terrible fights. At some point, her husband tells her to collect her stuff and leave. She collects her belongings and moves to her uncle's house, assuming it would be a short temporary departure. Several attempts at reconciliation fail. Bibi Khanum begins to fear that her husband might divorce her and that she would lose her children, especially as she had already forsaken her mahr, making divorce easy. At first, she was at a loss as to why her husband had become different toward her. Eventually, it transpired that, in her absence, her husband had contracted Banu as a sigheh wife. With family intervention, the couple reconciles, and Musa agrees to forgo Banu's remaining time on the sigheh contract and she is dismissed from service. Bibi Khanum returns to the marital fold and household sovereignty. This is where her autobiographical fragment ends, but it turned out not to be the end of Bibi Khanum's complicated marital life, as I have learned over the past two decades from her relatives, from her granddaughters, and from the memoirs of one of her daughters, Khadijeh Afzal Vaziri.[33]

The publication of Ma'ayib al-rijal had connected me to some of the Vaziri and Mallah relatives in the United States. Much to my surprise, one of the relatives once indicated that Musa Khan had a daughter, named Maryam, from his sigheh wife.[34] There was no such trace in Bibi Khanum's story. Working with Bibi Khanum's granddaughter, Mihrangiz Mallah, I had already learned that after reconciliation, Bibi Khanum and Musa Khan had one more son. But no daughter had been mentioned.

In my next communication with Mihrangiz, I queried about Maryam, since the two of us had worked closely to create a genealogy of her family, going back almost five generations. Mihrangiz at first seemed taken aback. She asked how I knew. I explained the circumstances; she confirmed that the information was accurate. We added Maryam to the genealogical chart: Maryam's mother's name? No one knew, she said; let us just call her Banu as well. We did.[35] The fuller story I heard from Mihrangiz's older sister, Mahlaqa Mallah, only in the summer of 2014.[36]

Possibly sometime around 1909, Bibi Khanum had arranged for another sigheh wife for her husband. The first one, as we saw, had been ended as part of their reconciliation. In 1907, Bibi Khanum had established a school for girls, Dushizigan (which means "girls"), in her own residence (in Paqapuq, near Muhammadiyeh Maydan), as was often done in the early years of new schools for girls. Her husband had been posted to Shiraz and had taken their adult sons with him. This made the household free of adult men and thus preserved the gender-homosocial norms (later to become a state regulation for having young girls in private home schools).[37] But a year later, Musa Khan returned to Tehran. He wanted his wife to shut down the school. Bibi Khanum had a different resolution: according to Mahlaqa Mallah, she rented another residence (in Guzar 'Ali, Pachinar) and moved her husband and sons there; "tired of marital duties" and wanting to devote herself fully to girls' education and other women's activities of the time, Bibi Khanum hired a

FIGURE 3.4. Family photo. Aunt Mari is the first person on the left. Source: http://www .qajarwomen.org/en /items/14129A47.html.

female domestic to become a sigheh to her husband and manage the other household. The school continued for another couple of years but was finally closed sometime around 1911.[38]

Afzal Vaziri talks elliptically in her interview about these years of her mother's life: "My mother had grown old, she was tired, the family had dispersed, family problems had occurred, every family has its own particular inner problems. . . . When my mother's school closed down, my sister opened a school and I continued to teach there and continue my own education as well."[39]

From this second sigheh marriage, a daughter was born, Maryam, who (unlike her forgotten mother) became fully integrated into the Vaziri and Mallah familial network, referred to by the next generation as Khaleh (Aunt) Mari. She appears in numerous family photographs (fig. 3.4).[40]

Yet there is much confusion on how Musa Khan's sigheh wives are remembered and recorded. When Mihrangiz Mallah's edited version of her mother's life was first published, we had included a sketch of these two mar-

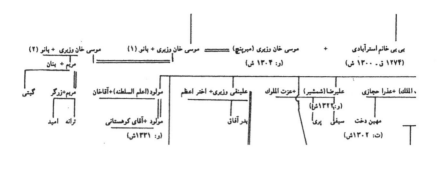

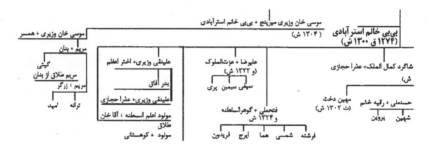

FIGURES 3.5 and 3.6. Genealogy fragment, prepared by Afsaneh Najmabadi with
Mihrangiz Mallah. Source: Author's drawing.

riages (fig. 3.5). A decade later, the text was revised by Mihrangiz and published in Tehran, with the first Banu disappearing from the modified genealogy (fig. 3.6). Figure 3.5 shows Musa Khan married to two different women,
named Banu, whereas figure 3.6 shows Musa Khan married to one woman,
referred to as spouse.

Possibly, Mihrangiz had assumed the two sighehs were only one and the
same woman—a rather unlikely coincidence, as these two marriages were
apart by nearly two decades. The first is reported in Bibi Khanum's text of
1894; very likely it was contracted in 1893, was ended by the dismissal of Banu
from the household, and no child was born of it.[41] The second marriage be-
longs to sometime around 1909–1910; Maryam was in fact only a few years
(b. ca. 1911–1912) older than Mahlaqa Mallah (b. 1917/1918). Regardless of
intentions, the erasure of the first Banu and preservation of the second, compounded by the unknownness of the names of either woman, generates the

effect that the second woman mattered for inclusion in the family's genealogy only because a child had been born, who had become part of the family. Furthermore, this inclusion comes at a price, so to speak: the second Banu's designation is transformed from sigheh into a more neutral term, spouse, as sigheh had become an affront to modern sensibilities. Yet this move, somewhat contradictorily, weakens the narrative of the Vaziri and Mallah families as modernists. It makes Musa Khan more strongly bigamous.

Several of Bibi Khanum's sons, Mihrangiz's uncles, had also married more than once. The dates of marriages and possible divorces were not indicated in the genealogy we had sketched. In response to my queries about whether these marriages overlapped or not, on two occasions, Mihrangiz emphasized that one wife had been divorced before the other marriage — polygamy was not practiced "in our family," she wrote.[42] Her grandfather, Musa Khan, had twice contracted sigheh wives; her father, Aqa Buzurg, had two (not sigheh) wives before Khanum Afzal (Khadijeh Afzal Vaziri) and another wife, Nusrat Zaman, when Khanum Afzal moved to Tehran. How had this sense of "our family as not polygamous" been generated into the next generation, against the known practices of family patriarchs?

Inclusions in and exclusions from who constituted the family were not consistently uniform but context dependent. In the interview with her son, as we saw, Khanum Afzal talks about her parent's five sons and two daughters; Maryam is thus not counted or mentioned in her entire oral narrative. Yet in so many photos, Maryam is included. So are Khanum Afzal's own husband's children from other marriages: Zubaydeh and Guli.

Mihrangiz noted that she had been surprised that her mother, in the taped interview, had not mentioned Maryam, or Guli, even though in her will she had insisted that Guli be counted as a sixth child and her house be divided equally among the six of them (three sons and two daughters of her own plus Guli). In fact, after Musa Khan's death (1925), according to Mahlaqa, Khanum Afzal brought Maryam and her mother to live with her; it was the same with not only Guli's integration into her household, but also Zubaydeh and her son. Zubaydeh's mother, Aqa Buzurg's first wife (name unknown), got a divorce and returned to her family. Khanum Afzal took care of Zubaydeh (eleven years of age when she had first moved to Naukandeh) into adulthood and marriage. After Zubaydeh's husband's death, she and her son Nusrat Allah became re-integrated into the Mallah household.

Changes across Class and Status Groups

The changes in meaning and purpose of marriage, along with the emerging dominance of the ideal of conjugally focused, affection-based, choice marriage happened not only within a short single generation, but also with various patterns among urban social groups. Consider the life story of Fari's mother, 'Alaviyeh Khanum.

'Alaviyeh Khanum, referred to by her children and grandchildren and great grandchildren as Khanum jun (lady dear), was the second wife of Badiʻ al-Saltaneh. Badiʻ al-Saltaneh (b. ca 1837/1838–d. 1920/1921) and his brothers were among the courtiers of Muzaffar al-Din Shah, since the latter's days in Tabriz as the crown prince. While in Tabriz, Badiʻ al-Saltaneh had first married the wife of his deceased older brother, Dabir al-Sultan—which was a common practice at the time. We do not know her name; from her first husband, she had had two daughters (Fatimeh Sultan and Khadijeh Sultan) and one son ('Ali Akbar Khan, who was granted the title Dabir al-Sultan later in life); she had four more daughters from Badiʻ al-Saltaneh (Sitareh, Ruqiyeh, Maʻsumeh, and Rubabeh).

When Muzaffar al-Din Mirza ascended the throne in 1896, Badiʻ al-Saltaneh moved with the new king to Tehran. Within a rather large square of Tehran, near the royal quarters (Arg), bounded in the north by Hasanabad Maydan and what became Sipah (now Imam Khomeini) Street, Farmanfarma Street (later Shapur, now Vahdat-i Islami) on the west, Mawlavi Avenue to the south, and the edges of Tehran Bazaar (Khayyam Street) to the east, the new king granted Badiʻ al-Saltaneh and his kin land, inclusive of residential and commercial properties (fig. 3.7). It was in this area where the entire familial group settled for years to come. In future years, they would purchase more buildings and shops in this area.[43]

Badiʻ al-Saltaneh's first wife seems to have passed away before the move to Tehran. There is no record or familial memory of her from the Tehran period of Badiʻ al-Saltaneh's life. With him came his large multifamily network, including his own four daughters from the first marriage and his deceased brother's children. Badiʻ al-Saltaneh's younger brother was Mirza Muhammad Khan (granted the title Vakil al-Dawleh in 1896).[44] In the same year, one of Vakil al-Dawleh's sons, Mirza 'Ali Khan, was also granted the title Dabir al-Sultan (formerly the title of his late uncle). He and his family also moved to Tehran with the new Shah and settled in the same neighborhood. Sometime

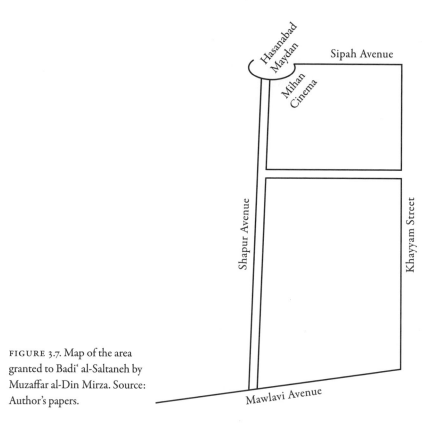

FIGURE 3.7. Map of the area granted to Badi' al-Saltaneh by Muzaffar al-Din Mirza. Source: Author's papers.

after Mirza Muhammad Khan's death, his title, Vakil al-Dawleh, was given to his son, and the title Dabir al-Sultan was transferred to the senior Dabir al-Sultan's son. Both of these junior figures we meet in the registration of Badi' al-Saltaneh's estate after his death: Vakil al-Dawleh as executor of the will, and Dabir al-Sultan as the guardian of his underage children. Subsequent to the move to Tehran, a complex pattern of intrafamilial marriages followed over the next generations (fig. 3.8).

Shortly before moving to Tehran, Badi' al-Saltaneh had married Khanum jun, from a prominent Tabrizi family, the Mir Mu'mins. Khanum jun's mother (Bibi jun), a sister, and three brothers all moved to Tehran as well (fig. 3.9).

All settled in the same area, between Hasanabad Maydan and Mawlavi Street. Khanum jun lived in the inner quarter (andaruni) of the Hasanabad residential complex. In addition to the andaruni, there was the outer quarter

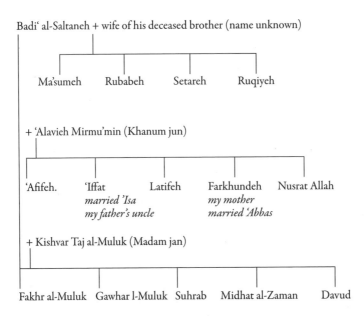

Badi' al-Saltaneh + wife of his deceased brother (name unknown)

Ma'sumeh   Rubabeh   Setareh   Ruqiyeh

+ 'Alavieh Mirmu'min (Khanum jun)

'Afifeh.   'Iffat   Latifeh   Farkhundeh   Nusrat Allah
            married 'Isa   *my mother*
            my father's uncle   *married 'Abbas*

+ Kishvar Taj al-Muluk (Madam jan)

Fakhr al-Muluk Gawhar l-Muluk Suhrab Midhat al-Zaman Davud

FIGURE 3.8. Genealogy of Badi' al-Saltaneh's immediate family. Source: Author's papers.

(*biruni*) and, in between the two sections, Badi' al-Saltaneh's private quarter (*khalvat*), which included as well all the household services (such as kitchen and storage basements) to serve both andaruni and biruni quarters.

Three years into his marriage with Khanum jun, around 1898–1899, Badi' al-Saltaneh married Kishvar Khanum (b. ca 1886–d. ca. 1951), who was given the title Taj al-Muluk upon marriage but called Madam jan by all the children. Apparently, Madam jan's brothers had been known to Badi' al-Saltaneh from Court circles in Tabriz. As one relative put it, "He had heard that they had a beautiful sister." She was settled in another house, in Birun-i Darvazeh Qazvin (which meant "outside the Qazvin Gate"). This neighborhood had been outside the city gates before the expansion of Tehran's perimeter and gates in 1868–1869; now it was part of one of the newly developed and more prestigious neighborhoods, Sangilaj. My mother, Fari, recalled that Taj al-Muluk's house was at the end of Shapur Street, on a side alley called Kucheh-i Aramaneh (alley of Armenians).

Madam jan's house had a biruni and an andaruni, but no khalvat, as was the case with many residences of the elite. In such cases, biruni also served the functions of the khalvat, as far as the patriarch's private socializing was concerned. Fari recalled that Madam jan was quite dear to her father, because

FIGURE 3.9. Family photo. The people in the photo: (*top to bottom*) Khanum jun, Bibi jun (*right*), Badi' al-Muluk (*left*), 'Iffat, Fari, Badi' al-Muluk's son. Source: http://www.qajarwomen .org/en/items/14128A1 .html.

after his numerous daughters — four from his first wife, followed by 'Alaviyeh Khanum's children, all girls (until the last one, a son born ca. 1914–1915), and Madam jan's first two girl children — finally a son was born (ca. 1905). Badi' al-Saltaneh named him Suhrab, after a family patriarch who had migrated from Georgia to Tabriz and from whose name eventually the entire family took its surname, Suhrabi. Suhrab, as the family lore went, inherited his father's Qur'an and ceremonial sword. Madam jan subsequently gave birth to a second son, Davud (1908–2008), and one more daughter (Midhat Zaman, b. ca 1912–d. ca. 2002).

The two wives could not have been more different. According to one of Fari's nieces — herself a religiously observant person — Khanum jun's family were *khushkeh-mazhab* ("dryly religious"). Born and brought up in Tabriz, Khanum jun was quiet by temperament and upbringing. Girls were encouraged to be sober, it is said. Her literacy was limited to reading the Qur'an, which was not uncommon. Children would learn to memorize the Qur'an first, and learning to read it was a memory aid.[45] After the death of her only son, Nusrat Allah, in 1936, Khanum jun became even more quiet and withdrawn.

Madam jan, on the other hand, was from a more sociable worldly circle of military men.[46] By all family members' accounts, she was a jolly social type, outgoing and rambunctious.

As mentioned earlier in this chapter, Khanum jun took in her husband's new marriage silently, by a sort of marital strike. Beyond the brief marital strike, Khanum jun never made a fuss about Madam jan. As was the practice at the time, Badi' al-Saltaneh spent time in each household—Fari remembered it as two or three days in Khanum jun's residence, the rest with Madam jan; another relative had heard that he spent lunchtime in Khanum jun's residence and evenings with Madam jan. In the last two years of his life, when his health was failing, he stayed entirely in Madam jan's house. Khanum jun's children would be taken to visit their father a couple of times a week, Fari recalled. He died there some time in 1339 AH (1920–1921). Seeing his body being washed in the courtyard was Fari's last visual memory of her father. From Khanum jun, four daughters and one son survived into adulthood. Madam jan had three daughters and two sons.[47]

One of Badi' al-Saltaneh's nephews, Mirza 'Ali Khan Vakil al-Dawleh, had been designated as his will's executor; another, 'Ali Akbar Khan Dabir al-Sultan, became the guardian of his five underage children, two daughters and three sons at the time of his death. With the four daughters from his first wife, there were nine adult daughters.

The two nephews began to sell much of their uncle's accumulated properties in Hasanabad to finance the life of his large number of children and his two widows. They refurbished the khalvat quarter and moved both wives and all the unmarried children to that part of the Hasanabad complex, and they began to sell all other properties, usually rented out at first on condition of a later purchase option and then purchased by the tenant—common at the time (fig. 3.10). It was in the refurbished khalvat part of the house that they all—Khanum jun, Madam jan, and all their unmarried children—lived in from sometime in 1922 until sometime in 1937.

The khalvat courtyard had a very large oval pool (hawz) in the middle. Khanum jun's first child had drowned in this pool, but the pool was also evocative of happy memories. They used to cover the hawz with wooden planks when there was a celebratory occasion; once when the children were playing and jumping up and down on the boards, one broke and they all fell into the hawz, with "the mothers"—as Fari would always refer to Khanum jun and Madam jan—scrambling to pull them out. On the northern side of the pool, there was a long and wide veranda, with two sets of stairs, one on

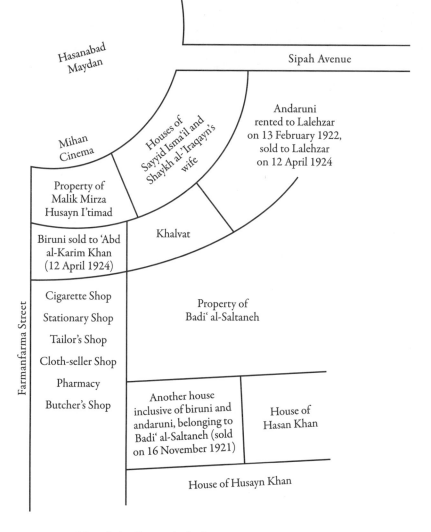

FIGURE 3.10. Map of sales. Source: Author's papers.

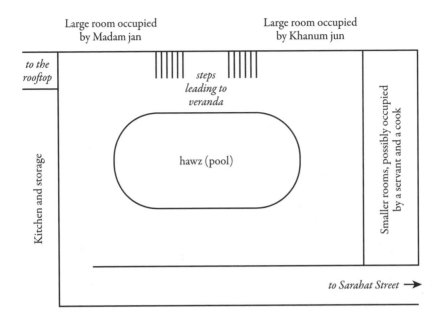

FIGURE 3.II. Sketch of the yard of the shared house. Source: Author's papers.

each end; the veranda covered the entire frontal south-facing windows of two large rooms, referred to as *talars*.

Each wife and her unmarried children were housed in one talar. On the western side of the pool, the kitchen and storage were located; there was also a ladder that would lead to the rooftop. Smaller rooms stood on the eastern side of the pool, possibly occupied by a servant and a cook. To its south, a wall separated the yard from a smaller yard that led to Sarahat Street (fig. 3.II).

Underneath the two talars, there were large basement rooms, possibly serving as storage in older times but now doubling as a refuge from summer heat. The children would spend their afternoons in one of these rooms, escaping not only heat but also the adults' demand that they ought to take a nap, playing until adults would wake up from their afternoon nap. There was a rotation of children eating their meals, all together, one week in one mother's room and the next in the other. Apparently, the relation between Khanum jun and Madam jan was courteous, but not intimate enough to share meals. As Fari recalled, "Now that their husband was dead, there was nothing to quarrel about." Yet she would add, "Of course there were occasional minor quarrels, between mothers and among siblings. That is some of the bitter memories of one's childhood." She remembered Madam jan fondly: "She liked me a great deal and asked for me often."

It was in the yard of this house that several photographs were taken that bore on the verso "with the whole family" (figs. 3.12–3.16). There are several ways that one can interpret this phrase. My initial reading in 2014, a moment intensely defined by the puzzle of my father's second family, was to see "the whole family" as the inclusivity of all the siblings and some children of the next generation, around the two senior women of the family—who happened to be co-wives, living together after their husband's death.

Taken on the first day of the Persian New Year, 21 March 1937, in the Hasanabad house, the ink dedication on the back of one photograph (figure 3.15) read "to my loving sister." This was in Nusrat Allah's handwriting. Born in 1914 or 1915, he was Fari's youngest brother, who died young, sometime in 1937. Fari always showed a sad air of reluctance to say much more about him. When she finally agreed to write some of her early life memories, and be interviewed in the 1990s, every time his name would come up, she would quickly move on to other topics. When discussing the early death of her first child, Farinaz, in 1943 (at just over a year old), Fari said that this had been the third terrible death for her: her father (she had been about nine years of age when he died ca. 1921), her brother, and her first child.

In addition to this dedication, in ink, the verso also bore a note in pencil, in 'Iffat's handwriting: "remembering first of Farvardin 1316 with the whole family." It must have referred, I imagined, to the fact that these photographs included all siblings, the two mothers, and some of their grandchildren.

This meaning of "with the whole family" had stayed with me until I learned that Nusrat Allah had not simply died; he had committed suicide, sometime in 1937. As the baby of the family and the only son Khanum jun gave birth to, he had been very dear to all his sisters, but he had a particularly close relation with 'Iffat, who was twelve years older than him. Now the distinctions, in color, writing utensil used, and in handwriting, on the back of these photographs suddenly told another story: 'Iffat may have, must have, added her penciled notation at a later date, after Nusrat Allah's suicide, as a way of remembering his living presence in these photographs.

The meaning of this single phrase, "with the whole family," and with it the meaning of the photograph, became more complex yet again, as I learned more about Khanum jun's life. After Nusrat Allah's suicide the complex family residence broke up. Several family members recalled that Khanum jun

FIGURES 3.12 and 3.13.
"With the whole family."
Source: http://www
.qajarwomen.org/en
/items/14128A17.html.

had insisted on moving out, saying she could not tolerate living in the same space in which Nusrat Allah had been present. They rented a house on Sha- pur Street; Khanum jun moved there with her two unmarried daughters, 'If- fat and Fari.

Madam jan moved to another rented house as well. "The whole family" were no longer together; indeed, I could not find a photograph that included all the kin in this photograph in later years. These family photographs nar- rate the changing practices of family lives—who counts as family, and how that changed within one generation.

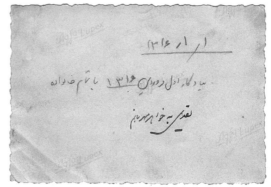

FIGURES 3.14–3.16.
"With the whole family."
Source: http://www
.qajarwomen.org/en/items
/14128A8.html.

Complex familial relations and marital conflict negotiations were not unique to the Suhrabis, of course. On my father's side of the family, until his generation, many married several times, at times sequentially but as often openly polygynously. The enlightened family patriarch, A'Shaykh Hadi, had two wives, Galin Baji and Sakineh Khanum; both lived in adjacent houses on Najmabadi Dead-end. As if a source of modernist embarrassment, as if his bigamy cast a shadow over his reputation as an enlightened cleric, the Najmabadis of my father's generation never tired of telling of A'Shaykh Hadi's unfailing practice of equity among his wives. After the construction of the two houses was complete, the story is told and retold, he took each wife separately to tour the two houses and at the end asked which house she would prefer to live in, to which the wife would respond in surprise "but the two are identical." As we will shortly see, his son, 'Abbas's grandfather, A'Shaykh Mahdi, married four times, two simultaneously and, later, two sequentially.

The complex and selective integration of wives and children into residential quarters is another lens through which one could trace the changing patterns of marriage and familial expectations.[48] In large urban families, marriages tended to be intrafamilial as we have seen. At times, a nonfamilial wife faced special challenges, including hostility on the part of her husband's relatives. We saw this even in 'Abbas and Fari's generation, but two generations earlier A'Shaykh Mahdi's third marriage seems to have generated a similar challenge.

He was called Aqa jun (dear sir) by his children, grandchildren, and great grandchildren; he was very beloved by them all. He was Nuri Khanum's father, living around the corner from 'Abbas and Fari. He frequently came to visit them; theirs was his daughter's residence after all. He passed away in 1957—when he was married to his fourth wife, Ashraf Khanum.

His first wife was Fatimah Sultan (1870–1906), a distant paternal third cousin. They had several children, but only one daughter, Huma (1900–1968), lived to adulthood. His second wife was Ruqiyah Kundushlu, a sister of his father's second wife, Sakinah Kundushlu. They married sometime in the early 1890s. Nuri (1895–1979), 'Ayni (1898–1936), Rubabeh (1900–1967), and Sadiqeh (1903–1955) were their daughters. His third wife was Zahra Malik Dawlatshahi. She passed away in 1949. They had two sons, Amir 'Imad al-Din (1917–1987) and Seif al-Din (1922–2016). Shortly after Zahra Malik's death, he married his fourth wife (see fig. 3.17).

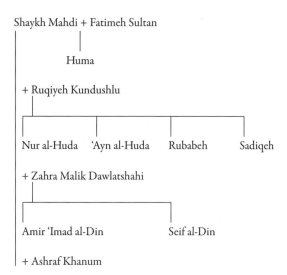

Shaykh Mahdi + Fatimeh Sultan
|
Huma

+ Ruqiyeh Kundushlu

Nur al-Huda   'Ayn al-Huda   Rubabeh   Sadiqeh

+ Zahra Malik Dawlatshahi

Amir 'Imad al-Din   Seif al-Din

+ Ashraf Khanum

FIGURE 3.17. Shaykh Mahdi Najmabadi's marriages. Source: Author's drawing.

Aqa jun's first two marriages were very much in the same style as most men in the large Najmabadi clan for several generations. There was a great tendency among the Najmabadis, even down to my father's generation, to marry other Najmabadis. Indeed, there was generally an unfriendly attitude, at times bordering on hostility, toward non-Najmabadi brides. Such wives often formed close friendships; there were many stories of kin snobbery, at times maltreatment. Fari and Pari, who was the second wife of Ziya' — both outsiders — became close friends. In Pari's case, the problem of outsiderness was compounded by her husband's status: Ziya' was considered a virtual usurper of the protected Najmabadi family name. The family name was claimed to be legally protected; anyone coming to the attention of the clan for adopting the Najmabadi family name would be taken to court to demand that they change their surname. In the case of Ziya', he had become a usurper through no legal responsibility of his own: his mother, 'Azra, was a Najmabadi, but his father was not. His birth certificate, issued on 27 February 1927, records his surname as Najmabadi, his father's first name as Muhammad Husayn, and his mother's as 'Azra, with no surname indicated for either.[49] Apparently, 'Azra had decided that her only son deserved a more prestigious family name than the surname of her husband's — Fallahi Damavandi.

Aqa jun's third marriage with a non-Najmabadi woman possibly generated distancing tensions along with disapproving gossip in the neighborhood. It is not clear if her royal genealogy accentuated or lowered the Najmabadi clan's snobbery toward outsiders. Zahra Malik, affectionately called Shajan (an abbreviation of Shahzadeh jan, which meant "Princess dear") by her children and grandchildren, was a Qajar descendant on both maternal and paternal lines. This was also her third marriage. She had separated from her first husband, Zahir al-Islam, after a son (Abu al-Fazl) was born—he died in childhood. She then married Dr. Abu al-Hasan Bahrami. They had three daughters: 'Alam Taj, Malik Taj, and Shams al-Taj. Dr. Abu al-Hasan Bahrami had been married to Zahra Malik Khanum's sister; they had four sons and two daughters. After her death, he married his wife's sister; as we have seen, that was not uncommon.

Sometime around 1914, after Dr. Bahrami's death, Shajan went to Aqa jun's registry, requesting that he would represent her in some inheritance dispute. Aqa jun took a liking to her and soon asked for her hand in marriage. Upon marriage, Shajan did not move into her husband's house or neighborhood. They lived in her residence, Bagh-i Malik, on Qalamistan Street, near today's Tehran Railroad Station. Both their sons were born there. Was this because the Najmabadi clan would not welcome her as a nonclan wife? Was it because her Qajar lineage enabled her a decisive influence over residency? Was it because he preferred to keep this marriage out of the neighborhood and its active rumor and gossip life? No one knows. But eventually Bagh-i Malik was sold and, with its proceeds, a new house was built on the southern corner of Najmabadi Dead-end, on Shaykh Hadi Street. This was a large residence, with andaruni and biruni, a yard with a small pool in the middle, several rooms, and large storage basements. Shajan moved there with her sons and her mother, Nigarzad. At various times, two of her maternal sisters, Malik Taj and Shams al-Taj, also lived in this household (see fig. 3.18).

This residency lasted for almost a decade. In 1932, Aqa jun with Shajan, Bibi (a sister of Aqa jun), Seif al-Din, and several other relatives went on a hajj pilgrimage. Upon their return, Shajan and Aqa jan rented a house in the Akbarabad area, then moved to a house on Shu'a' al-Saltaneh Street.

What were the reasons for the move out of the Najmabadi neighborhood? We don't know. The Najmabadi Dead-end house was sold to Aqa jun's daughter, Sadiqeh, who rebuilt it completely and lived there to the end of her life (1955), with her second husband, Ziya' (they married in 1944). Prior to this marriage and after her divorce from Dr. Ahmad, she had lived with her sister 'Ayni in Bastiyun, where they also had their practice (both were gyne-

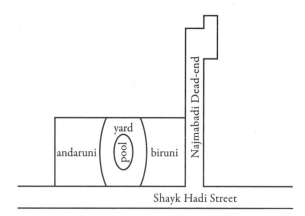

FIGURE 3.18.
Shajan's house in
the Najmabadi
neighborhood.
Source: Author's
drawing.

Najmabadi Dead-end

andaruni | yard | biruni

pool

Shayk Hadi Street

cologists). At times, after her divorce from her husband, Nuri had also lived with them.

From the sale of the house of Aqa jun and Shajan on Najmabadi Dead-end, a new residence was built off Hishmat al-Dawleh Street; from 1939, Aqa jun and Shajan, with their children and at times with one or another of her sisters, lived there. When Shajan passed away in 1949, the household broke up. By then the sons had married; Amir had already moved away, and now Seif al-Din and his wife, Shukuh Jamarani, also moved to new quarters near her father.

After Shajan's death, Aqa jun moved back to the Najmabadi neighborhood; shortly after, he married Ashraf Khanum. They lived in his sister's house. In later years, he moved in with his daughter, Sadiqeh, and died in her house in 1957.

Not only were Aqa jun's and Shajan's marriages and familial practices not anything close to being conjugally centered, but Shajan's mother's marriages were not simple affairs either. Nigarzad was the daughter of Shahzadeh Baygum (second daughter of Fath 'Ali Shah) and Sulayman Khan, a brother of Nasir al-Din Shah from the same mother, Mahd-i 'Ulya'. Her husband, 'Abd al-Husayn Mirza Dawlatshah, was the son of Mu'ayyad al-Dawleh Tahmasb Mirza. In addition to Nigarzad, after he was appointed as the chief of the police (gendarmerie) of Isfahan, he took two more wives in that city, 'Aliyah (with whom he had three sons) and Asiyah (with whom he had one son). Nigarzad did not accompany him to Isfahan and stayed in Tehran, living with her daughter Shajan.

Complicated and intertwined marriage practices — including women marrying their brother-in-law after their husband's death and men marrying their sister-in-law after a brother's death — were given knowns of life. Facing a co-wife was not an unfamiliar story for many urban or rural families of Khanum jun's generation; Fari had grown up in one such setting. But for her, and for her children, this was all history — until that phone call from Tehran.

4. Urban Transformations

Changing Size and Architecture of Houses

Urban transformations during the twentieth century impacted the conjugalization of family and its associated monogamy. As houses became, at least for some social groups, smaller, and more importantly they ceased to accommodate more than one generation, the resident family became more conjugally centered. Yet, as several urban ethnographers have shown, even with increased urbanization, dispersion of upper- and middle-class large families, and reduced sizes of residential spaces, at times smaller familial units would move into the same apartment block, each occupying one floor, thus preserving in the architectural layout its multigenerational, horizontally connected, character. Nonetheless, this configuration implied that each apartment was conjugally centered.

For lower economic classes that often shared a house in which multiple families lived, often each multigenerational family occupied one room around a central courtyard. These families became more couple-centered over this period. Judith Goldstein's example from Yazd, which relates the experience of the Jewish community there, could have been about many Muslim combined households as well. "Whereas only a generation ago it was not uncommon for five or six families to live together in one house, each family taking a room, today the nuclear family is the norm, and even that unit may have missing parts, because grown children often leave Yazd."[1]

Concurrently, the modernist aspiration for love-centered monogamy had generated a need for secrecy for men who took second wives, whether as a permanent marriage or as sigheh. The crowded and expanding city of Tehran and the changing habits of urban life provided the possibility of having two families in the same city, while keeping one unknown to the other. Tehran's population grew from 210,000 in 1922 to 540,000 in 1941, "with considerable growth of the city."[2] For 'Abbas's two families, as I learned later, there had been, at least through the mid-1940s, some overlapping family circuits between some of the Najmabadis and the Buluris (the family of my father's other wife, Mansureh). Giti, one of Mansureh's daughters from her first marriage, told me that, as a child, she had actually met my sister (Farzaneh) during a Persian new year visit to a common family acquaintance; no one had mentioned the connection between the two girls. There seems to have existed an unspoken rule of keeping secrets and staying silent that protected this knowledge from seeping across familial circuits, circulating in wider circles as gossip, and reaching my mother's ears. Upon the marriage of Mansureh and 'Abbas, this became an explicit promise to my father on the part of the second family not to inform the first, and that kept secret enabled 'Abbas to manage his complicated familial life in a single city, for almost two decades, from 1954 to when my parents moved to Karaj in 1971.

The transformation and rapid growth of urban centers such as Tehran were critical in making secret relations, including other marriages, possible. One's conjugal home in one neighborhood could look monogamous, while a second home in another faraway neighborhood was the abode of another family. With urban expansion, the breakup of closely knit, often kin-related, neighborhoods ruptured the circulation network of gossip, rumors, and information, making familial and social secrets possible. To paraphrase Georg Simmel, the secret produced an immense enlargement of life. The secret offered "the possibility of a second world alongside the manifest world." Yet, as Simmel also notes, "even where one of the two does not notice the existence of a secret, the behavior of the concealer, and hence the whole relationship, is certainly modified by it."[3] In some cases, he adds in a footnote, "this hiding has a sociological consequence of a peculiar ethical paradoxicalness. For however destructive it often is for a relation between two if one of them has committed a fault against the other . . . , it can, on the contrary, be very useful for the relation if the guilty one alone knows of the fault. For this causes in him a considerateness, a delicacy, a secret wish to make up for it, a yieldingness and selflessness, none of which would ever occur to him had he a completely untroubled conscience."[4] Was this also part of the emotional bond that 'Abbas had with my mother, Fari? He clearly loved her to the end of his life, and despite his other flirtations, she remained a significant part of his affective life. So did Mansureh.

Older communication circuits that would have made familial secrets nearly impossible were no longer efficient enough. Figures that were core characters of larger urban households and significant figures in familial information gathering included female servants, nannies, and wet nurses. As Simin Bihbihani writes of their old nanny and wet nurse, Tayeh Khanum, and her daughter, "were they alive today, they would have become newspaper reporters. Not a moment went by that they did not come with some news; who came, who left, who died, who got married, who had a baby son, who gave birth to a girl."[5] Neighborhood and family gossip generated critical knowledge.

Such knowledge was particularly important for a family's decision about a suitor's appropriateness for their daughter. Families began to resort to other modes of information gathering and background checking. In Kaukab's case, as we saw, her mother had demanded that the woman who had come to ask for her daughter's hand for a potential groom would swear on the Qur'an that he had no other wife, indicating that they did not know how else to gather that critical piece of information.

As an example of shrinking houses, as we saw in the previous chapter, after my maternal grandfather's death (around 1920–1921), his two wives were moved into one residential unit in Hasanabad, where they lived with their unmarried children until sometime in 1937. The building chosen for their residence has been his private quarter (the khalvat), not the inner or outer (the andaruni and the biruni) quarters. Those buildings, along with the rest of his properties, were slowly sold off to finance the life of his large number of children and his two widows. With this death and consequent residential move, a lifestyle and its associated domestic architecture came to an end for the Suhrabis.

Compared to her father's residence in Hasanabad, a mere generation later, Fari lived in a small, modest house. After 'Abbas finally succeeded in getting employment in Tehran in early 1943, he set out to repair his father's old house so that it could accommodate his young family. After the birth of their first child, Farinaz, relations with his mother, Nuri Khanum, improved; before the birth of the second child, they moved into 'Abbas's paternal house, sharing the residence with his father, Aqa'i. Soon Nuri, even without marital reconciliation with her husband, moved in with them.

The house was old and modest, a total of 140 square meters, inclusive of the middle yard. As one entered, a hallway (dihliz) took you to the small yard (fig. 4.1). On the hallway's right, as one entered the house was Nuri's room; Aqa'i's room was an attic under the roof (balakhaneh) on the same side of the building. Below there was a basement, simultaneously an escape from summer heat and a storage space. Across the yard, there was a kitchen, a

FIGURE 4.1. Family photo in which you can see the hallway that leads to a yard. Source: Author's album.

room for receiving guests (*mihmankhaneh*), and a set of stairs leading to my parents' room, which my sister and I shared with them. Even as my parents shared this house with my father's parents (after Aqa'i's death in 1948, only with Nuri), and even as Nuri was certainly the matriarch of the household, the house was now their conjugal abode, centered around Fari, 'Abbas, and their two children.

In the case of the Suhrabis, the transformation from a large, complex residence to a smaller unit was prompted by the death of the family patriarch; but it also coincided with a more general trend in urban socioeconomic and cultural changes in the late Qajar and early Pahlavi decades that transformed Tehran—including its neighborhood grid, its architecture of residential houses, the structure of its spaces for work, and the patterns of socializing practices and leisure activities.[6]

Urban Transformations of Home and Street

On a residential level, schematically speaking, the birunis became redundant and the andarunis became homes. But what happened to the khalvat, conceptually and in some of the elite residences as a third building complex?

To state the obvious, only in very affluent, elite residences, the concepts of an all-male working space, a familial living space, and the possible third space for male homosocial leisure activities of the family patriarch corresponded to actual physical buildings. In more humble houses, male leisure time would often be spent in teahouses, or in places of specific all-male fraternal practices, such as *takiyehs*, sufi lodges, and *zurkhanehs*. The living quarter, while following rules of gender comportment to the extent possible, were often female spaces during the day, if men worked outside the home. Women's leisure activities, beyond the ordinary pleasures of life usually combined with a day's work (such as doing work or going to the bath in a group), were organized around specific days, each of which had their own corresponding socializing space. In Tehran, for example, 27 Ramadan was spent in Imamzadeh Zayd; around mid-Sha'ban—celebrated by the Shi'is as the birthday of the twelfth Imam—visits to Hazrat 'Abd al-'Azim were popular. On the thirteenth of the new year, many gardens—initially outside city gates, but, when shifting of the Tehran moats occurred in 1867–1868, many relocated within the new Tehran perimeter and gates—were open to women's presence. Many memoirs of the period note at some length women's presence on these occasions and in these locations, before socializing habits began to change.[7]

But for the moment, and for following the transformation of the Hasanabad residence, I want to return to the points above: the birunis became redundant; the andarunis became modern homes; but what happened to the khalvat?

For urban, elite men, the birunis had served as formal workspaces (and for male socialization), especially for "men of state." As Ali Gheissari has aptly put it, "It was not the minister who would walk to the ministry but the ministry that would go to the home/office of the minister—it was within the minister's personal and private space that most of the meetings and the bulk of the paperwork of his ministry were handled."[8] Merchants' workspaces were often located in trade houses in the bazaar; seminaries and mosques also served as workspaces for men of religion.

In the last decade of the nineteenth century and the first decades of the twentieth, spaces of work and education for urban, elite men began to change. Previously, nonseminary education was carried out through home tutoring. However, the establishment of Dar al-Funun on 28 December 1851 marked the beginning of a shift in educational space, and for almost fifty years it remained the only institution of higher learning (except for the Military Academy). Then a number of schools were established during Muzaffar al-Din Shah's years.[9] Both for the students and the teachers, these were spaces that took them out of their homes, and this began to introduce alternative modes of socializing not only for work but also for leisure.

The establishment of offices for state business — such as the courts, office of finances and tax collection, office for customs, and so on — began a process of bureaucratization of the state in the late Qajar period, which was greatly accelerated under Riza Shah (r. 1925–1941). This too took elite men outside their birunis for work. So what used to be carried out in the birunis moved into offices; that included state affairs in courtiers' residences, life registries' work in local neighborhood notables, and nonseminary education and tutoring in the residences of learned men (and women) — all became bureaucratized, and their space of performance began to move into state buildings, schools, or various offices.

For some residences, transformation of work practice into a state-defined, or state-registered, activity required architectural transformations, turning part of the former biruni outward onto the street, so that it could serve as a publicly visible office. Shaykh Isma'il Najmabadi's neighborhood registry, *mahzar*, initially part of his biruni, had to become a registry office (with a state-assigned number), opening out onto 'Urfi Alley. A narrow passageway continued to connect it to the rest of his residential complex, whose andaruni now had its own entrance through Najmabadi Dead-end (fig. 4.2).

All the way through the 1950s and early 1960s, Najmabadi Dead-end was completely occupied by various clan members. Even several houses that were further away, off 'Urfi Alley, were occupied by Najmabadis. 'Abbas and Fari lived in a house at the end of 'Urfi Alley. As Mina Marefat has noted, many neighborhood dead-ends were familial passages among different kin houses.[10] The Najmabadi kids played childhood games, such as *gurgam bi-hava* (similar to tag) and *qayim mushak* (hide-and-seek), on these streets. They developed a sense of owning the streets and the neighborhood. This was *their* neighborhood and remains so, even as today only one house in the whole neighborhood remains occupied by a Najmabadi.

The birunis became redundant; the andarunis became home. What has been less often discussed is what happened to the khalvats, spaces of elite

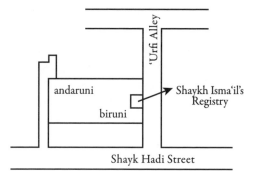

FIGURE 4.2. Transformation of birunis to accommodate for public access. Source: Author's drawing.

male socializing. In most houses, the andarunis became the familial space of home (*khaneh*), as the birunis began to become redundant as spaces of work, completing the urban split between work and life for this generation. Loss of the birunis went hand-in-hand with loss of the khalvat in the more elite, urban households.

More generally, the khalvats and at least some of the male homosocial leisure activities began to spill "out," unless they were familial sociality turning "in" onto the andaruni-become-home. As life in the andarunis became more gender-mixed, male socializing that was not folded into familial life moved toward street strolls, meeting in cafés that were the elite version of popular teahouses, and spending evenings in clubs, theaters, and cinemas that were the modernist elite's versions of zurkhanehs, takiyehs, and sufi lodges. On that level, these streets, cafés, clubs, and theaters were the equivalent of *patuqs* (hangouts) in more popular neighborhoods that Marefat has discussed. But on other levels, and aside from their obvious cultural class dimension, there were distinct spaces and practices. Most of the patuq spaces had been closed in; strolling was out there, in the open space of streets. Strolling was an act of leisure, passing time, with no evident purpose or end. It is this opening onto the public space of streets that impacted familial dynamics in specific ways. Furthermore, slowly perhaps but surely, these spaces became open to women's presence.

Concurrently, streets were no longer simply *ma'bars*, or passageways that often were winding narrow paths that connected different parts of a neighborhood; they became *kuchehs* (alleys) and *khiyabans* (streets). In other words, the khaneh and khiyaban emerged as urban twins. Even before the late 1920s into the 1930s, often referenced as a period of intense sociocultural transformations, a culture of street strolling as entertainment had begun to emerge in Tehran, with the well-known Laleh-zar and Amiriyeh streets as favorite locations.[11] Over and over again, the writers of memoirs during this time describe how, at the end of the workday, they would join friends for long strolls and engage in various entertaining activities (including going to theaters and later cinemas) before going home.

Memoirs and diaries of this period also provide us with more evidence of this generational shift. A published segment of Muhammad 'Ali Furughi's diaries, which covers a mere six months of his life in 1904, is nevertheless an excellent source for noting how from his father's generation to his own, the emergence of the higher education institutions as professional sites impacted his socializing daily routine.[12] He worked in several of the new schools, in some as a teacher and in others as an examiner.[13] On some days, he worked on a dictionary with his friend and collaborator Sadiq Hazrat, not in their birunis, but in one of the schools after their teaching hours. He would then regularly (almost daily) go to a bookseller/stationery shop to browse and purchase books, but also spend some time with other friends there—this shop, located on Nasiriyeh Street, clearly worked as a hangout for them.[14] They then would all go for a stroll, often all the way to the head of Laleh-zar Street.[15] His father also taught in some of the same schools but then went home and played backgammon with his regular partner, Aqa Muhammad Husayn, but at times joined by others. At their residence biruni, Furughi also helped his father with publishing the newspaper *Tarbiyat*.

It is tempting to consider this emerging male homosocializing public culture as an imported practice. Some of these men had visited Berlin or Paris. Some had not yet gone abroad, though they must have heard the circulating reports; they too became part of the strolling male public. But the changes in workspaces seem to have been more critical in the actual introduction of this daily routine than a mere Europeanization impulse, as we see in Furughi's case in 1904.

There seems to have been an emergent urban culture in these decades, at least in Tehran, whereby small circles of young (bachelor or not) male friends not only spent leisure time strolling certain streets and areas, but also engaged in relationships with women, prior to or even while becoming/being married to class-appropriate women.[16] Within this emergent socializing culture, some women (not only musicians and singers, as it is often believed) were participants. Although strolling started as an exclusively male activity, women strollers began to slowly make an appearance, causing much concern and public discussion.[17]

Women's street strolling, with no link to particular ceremonial ritual occasions, was a new phenomenon. Somewhat contradictorily, it was received both as an encroachment onto a space of male homosociality and as a welcome occasion for the men's voyeuristic (*tamasha*) pleasure, whereby they could ogle (*chashm charani*; "feasting the eye") women on the street, even though usually from a distance.[18] Despite much policing, spatially dividing the sidewalks into male and female sides as well as the police enforcement of the prohibition of male and female street mixing, women's claiming of these spaces for their own strolling pleasure became the subject of much critical debate, including in the pages of women's journals.[19] Nasim-i Shumal, under the title "Laleh-zar," devoted a long versified tale to the criticism of a young man flirting with a young woman on Laleh-zar Street, whose interpretation of liberty—now that they had a constitutional regime—was the freedom to exercise such behavior. The young woman told him off and lectured him otherwise.[20]

Some of the streets that became popular strolling spaces for women had indeed been in the vicinity of gardens or *imamzadehs* that previously were women's spaces on particular days, as mentioned earlier. These included Laleh-zar and Amiriyeh gardens, before their breakup and transformation into buildings and shops now lining Laleh-zar and Amiriyeh streets, or Tajrish, which housed Imamzadeh Salih. The most popular was Laleh-zar, with its shops catering to more Europeanized tastes.[21] The popularity of Laleh-zar is reflected in many writings of the period, including its being named as Tehran's Fifth Avenue and Champs-Élysées.[22]

Women's presence on the streets enabled a new mode of men's socializing with women who were not their kin. Some began to use words such as *rafiqeh* (a female friend with a sexual overtone), maîtresse, and others. Some of these relationships seem to have continued for several years, both before and after the man became matched and married. As we saw in chapter 3, some of these women, even those from very high-class Tehrani circles, became marked as prostitutes.

Such naming and marking seem to have been on one level a transitory practice, as more women joined the strolling public, and as the government took measures to regulate street mixing of unrelated men and women. On another level, the expression (and the related sentiment) of *zan-i khiyabani* (street woman) continued to circulate and make its mark on all women, becoming more a self-disciplining matter: how you dressed, where you went, with whom you went, how you talked and laughed in public—an etiquette of being an appropriate woman on the street emerged.

Several women of this later generation recall that they always went on these street strolls in groups. A memoir titled *Mahin Banu* spends many pages describing these outings:

> In the early 1930s, there wasn't much pastime activity. There were two cinemas, one on Laleh-zar street, the other on Firdausi street. When a film would come, we all went to it. We were a group of women, we were free during the day, we would get a ride to Istanbul [the name of a street in Tehran] and Laleh-zar. Laleh-zar was not a dirty street, as it has now become. It was a chic street, everyone would come all dressed up nicely, with make-up and decorations. Our fun was to go to Laleh-zar after ten in the morning, stroll from the bottom to the top of the street, Laleh-zar had become our *Champs-Élysées*. . . . Our pleasure was to look at the shops on both sides of the street. The Armenian and Jewish shops were really good. They would import everything. . . . There were also young men who would come to Laleh-zar. Everyone would choose one of them and thought of him as her love. . . . Some shop-keepers acted as go-between, taking messages and love letters between them. . . . [T]his was one of the ways men and women got to know each other, there wasn't any other way.[23]

As "other ways" of getting to know men became available, via workspaces, higher education institutions, and mixed-gender familial socializing, this function of mixed-gender street socializing may have become less significant, though it continued to remain a parental concern and material for works of fiction.

The Affective Life of Joint Households

The move to a joint household marked a downward mobility for the two widows of my mother's father. They previously had their own independent residential quarters. The financial strategy of simply selling properties to cover living expenses of the large family slowly eroded the financial standing and with it the social status of the entire family.[24] By the time Fari and her sisters had married, they were more accurately urban middle or even lower middle class, compared to their beginning status as urban elites. Some sisters and brothers had married richer relatives and acquaintances; for others, including my mother, the downward mobility was palpable. Fari's salary of an elementary schoolteacher and 'Abbas's salary of a Ministry of Agriculture civil servant barely covered their expenses. They ran a *nisyah* (credit) account with the local grocer. The account would be paid off at the beginning of each month, then by the middle of the month they had to switch from cash to nisyah again.

But at the time, Badi' al-Saltaneh's children were oblivious to the changing socioeconomics of the household. All the children and grandchildren of the two mothers, including Fari, Turan, Qamar, and Shamsi (a granddaughter of Khadijah Sultan), spoke of the years of joint living (1922–1937) as some of the happiest and most memorable years of their lives. "The whole family" was together.

Shamsi recalled the Hasanabad house as "the center of Suhrabi family life." In addition to siblings living in the house, others—including Mastanah, Turan, and Anushiravan Javan ('Adil Dawleh's three children from his first marriage), Shamsi and her younger sister Nayyir, and Khanum jun's and Madam jan's growing number of grandchildren—would spend extended time, at times many days, in the household. As Turan recalled, speaking of herself and her two sisters and two brothers, all living with her father, 'Adil al-Dawleh, and Gawhar al-Muluk in a nearby house in Amiriyeh, they "spent a lot of time with the other kids in the Hasanabad house."[25]

The children played together, ate together, and shared the basement giggles of summer afternoons and the rooftop pleasures of summer nights. Among the latter was watching the latest silent movie from the rooftop, which overlooked the yard of Mihan Cinema. When a new film was screened at Mihan, all the kids would converge at the house for dinner and watch from the rooftop. Once a large vinegar jug rolled off—some attributed it to the restless Suhrab—from their roof on to the audience, seated in the yard; that put an end to their free showtime. Everyone recalled the vinegar-jug disaster!

Mihan is listed as one of the first six or seven cinemas established in Tehran. In later years, the southeast side of Hasanabad Maydan was turned into a mini-bazaar (*bazarcheh*); in the 1960s, some of these shops were acquired by Bank Melli of Iran. The former proximity and the memories of the shared nights of movie watching seem to have generated a sense of proprietorship over that part of the southeastern crescent of Hasanabad Maydan. The continued sense of proprietorship on the part of the Suhrabis made them protest, futilely, the tearing down of the old structures and their replacement by a glass-and-concrete multistory building in 1964 (see figs. 4.3–4.5).

Suhrab seems to have been a particularly mischievous adolescent. Fari recalled that he had once mobilized some kids to go and attack their Jewish

FIGURE 4.3. Old Hasanabad Maydan. Source: Author's papers.

neighbor; in his adolescent years targeting Jews had become his idea of "fun." Apparently, the neighbors were engaged in some ritual. The timing proved almost catastrophic: it coincided with 15th Sha'ban that year (according to the Shi'ites, the birthday of the twelfth Imam); their Jewish neighbors were burning all leavened bread in anticipation of Passover. Suhrab had thought that the neighbors were burning an effigy of the Imam. Khanum jun rushed out and stopped the kids, explaining to them that it was a Jewish ritual. This story brings to life an otherwise ordinary financial document. Among all the transactions that Badi' al-Saltaneh's nephews engaged in to finance their uncle's heirs, one concerns the building that had served as the inner quarters (andaruni) of the Hasanabad residence. It was first rented, and subsequently sold—a common practice then and to the present day—to "Lalehzar, son of Jewish Ilisanan (kalimi)."[26] The former andaruni was still connected to the former khalvat, by a gated passageway that only later was fully blocked. This rental-sale document comes to life when "heard" through a story told all these years later, seeing a Jewish family next door, with their Muslim neighbor's children running around excitedly, planning to go and trash their feast.

FIGURE 4.4. Hasanabad Maydan, as rebuilt in 1964. Source: Author's papers.

FIGURE 4.5. Hasanabad Maydan, as refurbished in 2000. Source: Author's papers.

Among Fari's fondest memories, in addition to games and giggles, was the whole family going to the bath together. "One of my uncles had a bath built in his house. Whenever they would fire [heat] the bath, all of us would go over to his place. Mothers and girls together. We loved it. We were a joyous bunch." This was a full-day event, from "nine in the morning" until "three in the afternoon." All sisters, she said, would also go to the local mosque every night in Ramadan after the fast break. Watching Muharram processions from the rooftop was also remembered as a childhood joyful event, as if it were a passing-by carnival.

Strong childhood friendships emerged among the younger children and grandchildren in the joint household. Qamar recalled that she and Minoo Javan (Gawhar al-Muluk's daughter) were very close and remained so through their teenage years.[27] They hung out and went places together — "we were very *shaytun* [naughty] and noisy together," Qamar recalled. Indeed, Minoo's father would permit his daughter to roam the city only if she was in Qamar's company. Later years took Minoo and Qamar in very different directions. Minoo Javan became a well-known singer. Qamar married Ahmad Nadim, from an observant Muslim family who made it a condition of their marriage for Qamar to observe hijab. She agreed, creating much familial unhappiness among the Suhrabi sisters. As Qamar told the story, she had been determined to never marry, possibly looking at the unhappy marriages around her, including her aunt Badi' al-Muluk's and her mother's first two marriages. She rejected suitors until Ahmad Nadim, a young lawyer acquaintance of 'Isa ('Iffat's husband) asked for her hand. In the early 1940s, 'Isa used to rent a summer house in Damavand to escape Tehran's heat; the Suhrabi sisters and their children would all spend extended time there. Nadim was a colleague of 'Isa in the Endowment Office and visited frequently, meeting the un-hijabed Qamar in these outings. When he talked to her about marriage, she had at first been resistant but then considered that not marrying was not an option for long. He seemed like a reasonable man. She agreed, and she agreed to his condition. The Suhrabi sisters had embraced the unveiling order of 1936; Qamar's mother, Latifeh, and several of her aunts were professional women. For almost a decade, none had been observing the hijab. There was shock and dismay all around. Qamar herself was not a strictly observant Muslim, after all. 'Iffat lost several nights of sleep over Qamar's decision. For that first generation of women who had made the transition to professional life, with no hijab observance, the idea of a young, educated woman accepting to "go back" to chador was a loathed anathema. 'Iffat and her sisters, even before the official 1936 ordering of public unveiling, had not observed hijab at home. Eventually, everyone came to accept Qamar's decision. She was married around 1946–1947, at sixteen years of age. She moved into Nadim's large familial household in the Maydan Shah area, where Nadim's father's wife (also called Khanum jun), several unmarried brothers, and one sister all lived. She quit high school but later finished her education at a night school in the 1950s, after her three children had grown up. For Qamar, the decision was at the beginning just a matter of necessity; in some of the family pictures from the early years of her marriage, she is barely keeping her chador on her head. But then she became interested in studying Islamic teaching more intensively and eventually became an Islamic educator herself, holding classes starting in the 1960s until 2019.

The intimacies developed in the Hasanabad residence through shared daily life experiences — accidents, pleasures, and hazards — at times provided such a strong sense of kinship, akin to ties created by blood, milk, or marriage.[28] When Turan and Davud (eighteen years her senior) got married, there was a sense of discomfort in the family, as if Davud had married his niece — a forbidden marriage in Islam. Turan was the younger daughter of 'Adil al-Dawleh from his first marriage; she grew up in the household of his second wife, Gawhar al-Muluk, Davud's sister, whom Turan had called mother. Her birth mother had passed away at childbirth when her youngest brother was born. In Fari's memoirs, she writes, "Davud married his niece almost [*taqriban ba khvarzadah-ash izdivaj kard*]." Turan and Davud were not related by blood, but Turan had grown up in the Gawhar al-Muluk and 'Adil al-Dawleh household, so she had shared with Davud Hasanabad resident experiences.[29] Qamar as well recalled their marriage as confusing, especially to the younger children who were sure that an uncle had married a niece. Turan continued to think of Gawhar al-Muluk as her mother.[30]

All the children went through the modern school system. Fari talked about how her father was progressive and sent all of them to school. Madam jan's two older daughters, Gawhar al-Muluk and Fakhr al-Muluk, initially attended Tarbiyat School for Girls (located at the time in the nearby Bazarcheh Aqa Shaykh Hadi quarter), and her sons, Suhrab and Davud, went to Tarbiyat School for Boys (fig. 4.6).[31]

After Badi' al-Saltaneh's death and Madam jan's move to the shared Hasanabad residence, all the girls continued their educations at Namus, which Badi' al-Muluk, 'Iffat, Latifeh, and Fari also attended. All the girls finished high school and went to work as educators (except for the oldest daughter,

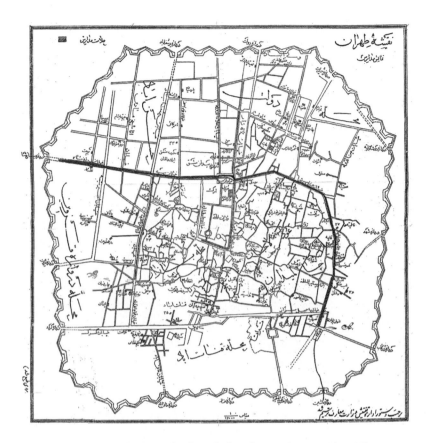

FIGURE 4.6. Location of Tehran schools marked on the map. Source: *Atlas-i Tihran-i qadim*, ed. Reza Shirazian (Tehran: Intisharat-i Dastan, 2015), 140–141.

Badiʿ al-Muluk, who had already married during her father's lifetime). All three sons graduated from Karaj School of Agriculture. The shared educational experiences further consolidated their sense of familial belonging, but as the children grew up and got married, they moved out.

The combined effect of these urban transformations meant that affective bonds were now as likely, if not more likely, to be formed among nonkin rather than siblings and cousins. Children were more likely to play with neighbors' children and schoolmates, rather than kin who shared a large joint household. As smaller houses became conjugally centered, affective ties also shifted to a more couple-centered pattern.

Epilogue

Naming Marriage, Naming Kin

The shift in meaning of marriage, from a household-centered merging of two familial groups (at times already intimately related) to a conjugal, couple-centered one, is reflected in several linguistic changes.

The older everyday expression for getting married was ta'ahhul (forming a household), and a married man was usually referred to as *muti'ahhil*. Among many families, the concept of *vaslat ba khanivadeh* — becoming connected with another family — continues to define a marital union. The shift to the increasing use of *izdivaj* (becoming coupled) for getting married itself reflects in language a shift in the meaning of marriage toward conjugalization.[1] Both concepts continue to circulate and produce marriage at once familial and individual.

Concurrently, kin vocabulary changed, making the relation to the conjugal couple defining of who is kin and how. More often than not, today in Persian the word *na-tani*, literally meaning "not of one body," is used to separate full and half siblings.

Fari never referred to her (half) siblings as na-tani. In her memoirs, writing about the years of co-residence of "the whole family" in the Hasanabad house, she refers to her mother and her father's other wife as "the mothers," or "the two mothers," never referring to one as a negation of something (*na-madari*). Nor did the grandchildren grow up calling different aunts and uncles differently, some as na-tani aunts and uncles. This turned out to be a linguistic pattern that was common among all the families I studied for this project. Some objected to its use even in our contemporary conversations.

Similarly, Mihrmah Farmanfarmayan, from the large Farmanfarma household, uses "our mothers," "my sisters and brothers," to refer to the numerous wives and children of her father, with no distinction of appellation among tani and na-tani. She explains that after her father's death, her mother,

Batul Khanum, lived in her own house and "one of her joys was to receive Farmanfarma's children. . . . [T]he relation with the older ones [these were already old by the time she joined his household] was formal but friendly, with those who grew up in the old andaruni . . . there was a special affectionate bonding. This was a reciprocal affection. Everyone, even the older ones, frequently visited her and addressed her as Maman jan."[2] Batul Khanum had been especially close with one of the other wives, Ma'sumeh Khanum, who, after Batul Khanum's death, had told Mihrmah losing her was more difficult than losing her sister.

In these large households, there is also the attachment generated with nonkin, especially with one's *naneh* (nanny) and *dayeh* (wet nurse). In Mihrmah's case when her naneh was sent away, she was so devastated that her mother started to take her to her own bed and to pay special attention to her.[3]

Another woman's memoir, *Mahin Banu*, echoes the same sentiment. Growing up together in large households generated a sense of kinship not primarily defined through blood and biological connections. Other wives of a father, in part by virtue of being mothers of one's brothers and sisters, became named as one's mother: "The relationship among us [all the children from her father's many wives] with our mothers was good; we didn't have any problem. With brothers and sisters, we did not have tani [full] and na-tani [half]. . . . [W]e considered all his wives like our own mothers, because we had brothers and sisters from all of them."[4]

In Qajar-period documents, in particular legal ones, such as inheritance divisions, wills, and family transactions, if a distinguishing clarification was necessary, it would be explicitly added as such: *batni*, meaning from the same womb/stomach, or *sulbi*, siblings who shared only a father. The *not*-belonging (as in the expression na-tani) would not be noted. Even beyond legal documents, we find various vocabulary but none referencing the distancing negation of *na-*.

Discussing the contentious complications that ensued after his father's death, when siblings began to work out the implementation of their father's will and division of family properties, 'Ayn al-Saltaneh refers to his batni and sulbi sisters.[5] Reporting on the death of his niece, in an entry dated 8 February 1909, he refers to her as the batni sister of Fakhr al-Mamalik (Ardalan).[6]

Writing in her travelogue about her two "full" brothers, a Qajar princess (we do not know her name) refers to them as her mother-father brothers (*baradar-i madar pidari*), in contrast to two other much younger brothers who were born from her father's later second marriage.[7]

In other contexts, the actual chain of relationship would be explicitly stated. No general equivalent of a "step-" relationship existed. "Hishmat al-Dawleh's wife's daughter" would indicate a stepdaughter.[8] "Zan aqa-yi Aqa 'Ali" meant Aqa 'Ali's father's wife.[9] "The younger brother of the bride's father's wife [*baradar-i kuchak-i zan pidar-i 'arus*]" would translate into English as "step-uncle."[10]

This style of relational naming signifies the importance of the exact line and nature of connection—something critical to the question of who could marry whom. Turan, who was the daughter of one of Fari's sister's husbands from his first marriage, was fully integrated into the Hasanabad household as a maternal cousin (*dukhtar khaleh*). Her marriage to Fari's brother Davud created confusion among the younger generation over the permissibility of their marriage. Calling her the daughter of Gawhar al-Muluk's husband would have acted as a clarifying yet distancing naming.

The distancing vocabulary was at times used to that very effect, in circumstances where the marital relation to the head of the household, for instance, was noted without the expectation of, indeed with an intent against, the new wife becoming fully part of the larger household. When Haj Mirza Hadi Dawlatabadi's wife of a lifetime became ill and bedridden (she passed away in 1905/1906 [1323 AH]), he was already close to seventy years old. To help with his care, a young girl, Marziyeh Zamani, possibly a distant relative and perhaps eleven or twelve at the time, was brought to the household. A sigheh contract was performed with him to make her intimate labor licit. Upon this move into the Dawlatabadi household, she was named Munis-i Aqa (often pronounced Munis Aqa), literally meaning the companion of Aqa. This turned out to be more than a marriage of convenience, or a sigheh of *mahramiyat*; before Aqa's death in 1908/1909 [1326 AH], they had two daughters, Qamar Taj and Fakhr Taj. Nonetheless, she was never named as Haj Mirza Hadi Dawlatabadi's wife and remained Munis Aqa.[11] Indeed, after her husband's death, Sadiqeh Dawlatabadi, the daughter of Haj Mirza Hadi Dawlatabadi from his first marriage, took over the upbringing of her two much younger sisters and worked very hard to disconnect them from their mother. Munis Aqa was soon married off and out of the Dawlatabadi household.

In households where, unlike those of the Farmanfarmas or Fari's, one's father's wives were not all named mothers, expressions such as *zan aqa*, or later *zan pidar* (father's wife) was used. "Zan pidar" has entered contemporary kin vocabulary with a heavy negative load.

When did an expression such as "na-madari" (not mother, or stepmother) replace "zan aqa"? It is not possible to pinpoint a time, and different usages continue to the present. Quite possibly, living in a common residential unit and growing up together generated this nondistinction and the common vocabulary that marked them. Did the vocabulary begin to change as urban transformations resulted in the breakup of large residences into individual households, centered on the conjugal couple?

Zanjani, in his autobiography, written in 1927 or 1928 when he was about seventy-two years old, does use "na-madari," discussing the distance his kids felt toward the new wife he had married after the death of his first wife.[12] Whereas Khanum Afzal, in her 1974 interview with her son, refers to her husband's (half) brother as "Aqa's brother," in Mihrangiz Mallah's edited version of Afzal Vaziri's narrative (first published in 1996), he is referred to as "his na-tani brother."[13] On the other hand, Nasrin, Mahlaqa Mallah's daughter, strongly objected to the use of such vocabulary as "na-tani." She never felt, she noted, that anyone in the family considered in any form Maryam (Aunt Mari) not part of the family, and as we saw, Maryam was included in many family photographs.[14]

Mahin Banu, as we saw, emphasizes that siblings did not differentiate among themselves as tani/na-tani and they considered all the wives as mothers. Nevertheless, in other contexts of her memoirs, she does use "na-tani" and other distancing expressions such as not from the same mother (*az mother juda*).[15]

With the "imperial hegemony" of marrying for love and the conjugal ("nuclear") family as the ideal family, the emerging expressions for marriage and kin became the only expressions circulating in Persian.

NOTES

IN LIEU OF AN INTRODUCTION

1. Nancy Miller, "Putting Ourselves in the Picture: Memoirs and Mourning," in *The Familial Gaze*, ed. Marianne Hirsch (Hanover, NH: University Press of New England, 1999), 51–66, quotes from 51.

2. Deborah Cohen, *Family Secrets: Living with Shame from the Victorians to the Present Day* (London: Viking, 2013), 122.

3. Arafat Razzaque, "The Sin of Ghība in Early Islamic Thought: The Zuhd Tradition, Late Antique Religion, and Ibn Abī l-Dunyā's Book on the Ethics of the Tongue" (PhD diss., Harvard University, 2020).

4. Letter of 16 September 1996.

5. The URL of the manuscript is http://www.qajarwomen.org/en/items/14129A59 .html (accessed 11 May 2021).

6. Richard Péres-Penā, "Reporting the Reporting, Step by Step," *New York Times*, 1 April 2017, A2.

7. Michael Taussig, *Defacement: Public Secrecy and the Labor of the Negative* (Stanford, CA: Stanford University Press, 1999), 137.

8. Arlette Farge, "The Honor and Secrecy of Families," in *A History of Private Life*, vol. 3: *Passions of the Renaissance*, ed. Roger Chartier, trans. Arthur Goldhammer (Cambridge, MA: Harvard University Press, 1989), 571–607, quote from 582.

9. Alain Corbin, "Backstage," in *A History of Private Life*, vol. 4: *From the Fires of Revolution to the Great War*, ed. Michelle Perrot, trans. Arthur Goldhammer (Cambridge, MA: Harvard University Press, 1990), 457–667, quote from 469.

10. Michael Amico, "The Forgotten Union of the Two Henrys: A History of the 'Peculiar and Rarest Intimacy' of the American Civil War" (PhD diss., Yale University, 2017), 352.

11. From Michael Amico's email to author, 12 May 2017, emphasis in original.

CHAPTER 1. MARRYING FOR LOVE

1. This quote came from a videography produced by Soheila Rafeizadeh and Safoura Rafeizadeh in 1990.

2. This quote is from Giti Afruz's third notebook, p. 26, 23 April 1945 (3 Urdibihisht 1324). All translations from Persian are mine, unless otherwise noted. The first and second of her notebooks are available online: http://www.qajarwomen.org/en/items/1251B78 .html. I thank Giti Aruz for giving me access to the third notebook.

3. Simin Bihbihani, *Ba madaram hamrah: Zindigi-namah-'i khudnivisht* (Tehran: Sukhan, 2011), 320–321.

4. The literature on the topic is rich and large, including Kenneth Cuno, *Modernizing Marriage: Family, Ideology, and Law in Nineteenth- and Early Twentieth-Century Egypt* (Syracuse, NY: Syracuse University Press, 2015); Beth Baron, "The Making and Breaking of Marital Bonds in Modern Egypt," in *Women in Middle Eastern History: Shifting Boundaries in Sex and Gender,* ed. Nikki R. Keddie and Beth Baron (New Haven, CT: Yale University Press, 1991), 275–291; Beth Baron, *Egypt as a Woman: Nationalism, Gender, and Politics* (Berkeley: University of California Press, 2005), especially chapter 1; Judith E. Tucker, *Women in Nineteenth-Century Egypt* (Cambridge: Cambridge University Press, 1985); Beshara B. Doumani, *Family Life in the Ottoman Mediterranean: A Social History* (Cambridge: Cambridge University Press, 2017); Alan Duben and Cem Behar, *Istanbul Households: Marriage, Family and Fertility, 1880–1940* (Cambridge: Cambridge University Press, 1991); Amy Motlagh, *Burying the Beloved: Marriage, Realism, and Reform in Modern Iran* (Stanford, CA: Stanford University Press, 2012); Hanan Kholoussy, *For Better, for Worse: The Marriage Crisis That Made Modern Egypt* (Stanford, CA: Stanford University Press, 2010); and Guity Nashat, "Marriage in the Qajar Period," in *Women in Iran: From 1800 to the Islamic Republic,* ed. Lois Beck and Guity Nashat (Urbana: University of Illinois Press, 2004), 37–62. For a discussion of companionate marriage in the press of early decades of twentieth-century Iran, see also Camron Amin, *The Making of the Modern Iranian Woman: Gender, State Policy, and Popular Culture, 1865–1946* (Gainesville: University Press of Florida, 2002), chapter 5, "Renewal's Bride." Mytheli Sreenivas's book *Wives, Widows, Concubines: The Conjugal Family Ideal in Colonial India* (Bloomington: Indiana University Press, 2008) offers a brilliant analysis of similar emergences in India.

5. Elizabeth A. Povinelli, *The Empire of Love: Toward a Theory of Intimacy, Genealogy, and Carnality* (Durham, NC: Duke University Press, 2006).

6. Povinelli, *Empire of Love,* 2–3.

7. Povinelli, *Empire of Love,* 3–4.

8. Povinelli, *Empire of Love,* 17.

9. Povinelli, *Empire of Love,* 183.

10. Povinelli, *Empire of Love,* 198.

11. I use "generationally expansive household" instead of "extended family." As Naomi Tadmor noted some two decades ago, the concept of an "extended family" is misinforming of the familial concepts that would make sense to those whose familial practices we so name. It presumes a nucleated family as a core concept, in relation to which some have extensions beyond the core. Naomi Tadmor, "The Concept of the Household-Family in Eighteenth-Century England," *Past and Present* 151 (May 1996): 111–140. For eighteenth-century England, she suggests the use of "household-family" and argues that the notion of extended family "rests on the concept of the nuclear family, and particularly the conjugal

unit. Thus, for example, households that include relatives beyond the nuclear core are defined as 'extended,' . . . in the eighteenth century, families could exist quite apart from notions of conjugality. . . . The concept of the household-family . . . enables us to question the usefulness of the term 'extended family'" (133).

12. Baron, *Egypt as a Woman*, 22.

13. Mari Ladieh-Fuladi, *Jam'iyyat va siyasat dar Iran: Az mashruteh ta jumhuri-yi Islami* (Tehran: Mu'asseh-i Mutali'at-i Jam'iyat Shinasi Faranseh, 2003), 56.

14. Ladieh-Fuladi, *Jam'iyyat va siyasat dar Iran*, 79. For Egypt and Istanbul, see Cuno, *Modernizing Marriage*; and Duben and Behar, *Istanbul Households*.

15. "The fear that polygamy might increase the spread of venereal diseases among women of childbearing age became a powerful reason to deliberate the salutary virtues of monogamy." This quote is from Firoozeh Kashani-Sabet, *Conceiving Citizens: Women and the Politics of Motherhood in Iran* (New York: Oxford University Press, 2011), 67. Kashani-Sabet extensively discusses how, in the late Qajar era, "the purported erosion of marriage as an institution appeared connected to the moral laxity of Iranian society. The spread of venereal disease, accompanied by a perception of increased sexual promiscuity, reinforced the sense that Iranian society was becoming socially decadent" (53). The concern about the perceived effects of the spread of sexually transmitted diseases was implicitly linked with "the socially explosive issues of adultery and polygamy," which were skirted in explicit discussions (91). The connection between citizens' sexual health, a healthy population growth, and monogamy may have been skirted in explicit discussions since polygyny was a male prerogative that men seemed reluctant to give up. Jasamin Rostam-Kolayi discusses at great length how the journal *'Alam-i nisvan* covered the connection between arranged, sigheh, and polygynous marriages with the spread of venereal diseases in her chapter, "Expanding Agendas for the 'New' Iranian Woman: Family Law, Work, and Unveiling," in *The Making of Modern Iran: State and Society under Riza Shah, 1921–1941*, ed. Stephanie Cronin (New York: Routledge, 2003), 157–190.

16. Ahmad Khan was said to have gone to France and sought cure, and from his second marriage he had several children.

17. Mut'a marriage, marriage for (usually male) pleasure (tamattu'), is often translated into English as "temporary marriage," because the contract has an end date. There is no divorce, and unless renewed, it ends on that pre-arranged date. In Iran, the expression used is usually *sigheh*, literally meaning "contract." I am using *mut'a* or *sigheh*, and staying away from "temporary marriage," because its primary distinction in the past was that the purpose of the marriage was (usually male) pleasure and not forming a family. One of the changes over the period of my consideration, and linked with the changing idea of the ideal marriage, was the shifting of emphasis from pleasure to the timed character of sigheh marriage. In this process, it also became equated to prostitution in modernist discourse.

18. Svetlana Boym, *The Future of Nostalgia* (New York: Basic Books, 2001), xv.

19. Heghnar Zeitlian Watenpaugh, "The Harem as Biography: Domestic Architecture, Gender, and Nostalgia in Modern Syria," in *Harem Histories: Envisioning Places and Living Spaces*, ed. Marilyn Booth (Durham, NC: Duke University Press, 2010), 232.

20. Boym, *Future of Nostalgia*, xvi.

21. Boym, *Future of Nostalgia*, xvii.

22. Afsaneh Najmabadi, *Women with Mustaches and Men without Beards: Gender and Sexual Anxieties of Iranian Modernity* (Berkeley: University of California Press, 2005), chapter 6.

23. Shaykh Ibrahim Zanjani, *Khatirat-i Shaykh Ibrahim Zanjani: Sar'guzasht-i zindagani-i man*, ed. Ghulamhusayn Mirza Salih (Tehran: Kavir, 2001), 195. On Talibuf, see "Ṭālebuf, ʿAbd-al-Raḥim," *Encyclopaedia Iranica*, accessed 24 June 2021, http://www .iranicaonline.org/articles/talebuf. For *Siyahatnamah-i Ibrahim Bayg*, see "Ebrāhīm Beg," *Encyclopaedia Iranica*, accessed 24 June 2021, http://www.iranicaonline.org/articles /ebrahim-beg.

24. For a detailed discussion of some of the most important novels of this genre, see Claus Pedersen, *The Rise of the Persian Novel: From the Constitutional Revolution to Reza Shah 1910–1927* (Wiesbaden: Harrassowitz Verlag, 2016), chapter 5, "Socialist Realist Novels."

25. M. Ghanoonparvar, "Ḥejāzi, Moḥammad Moṭiʿ-al-Dawla," *Encyclopaedia Iranica*, accessed 24 June 2021, http://www.iranicaonline.org/articles/hejazi. See also Houra Yavari's discussion of Hijazi's work and its popularity, especially in the 1920s into the 1940s, in "Fiction, ii(b). The Novel," *Encyclopaedia Iranica*, accessed 24 June 2021, http://www .iranicaonline.org/articles/fiction-iibthe-novel.

26. Motlagh, *Burying the Beloved*, 14. This almost pales in comparison to Kasravi's critique of much of Persian classical literature, in particular when it comes to the subject of love, or 'ishq. See his *Dar piramun-i adabiyat* (Tehran: Firdaus, 1999), 125–142.

27. Murtiza Mushfiq Kazimi, *Tihran-i makhauf*, 5th ed. (Tehran: Ibn Sina, 1961), 27. For a discussion of this book's cultural significance through the lens of trans-spatalization, see Rasmus Christian Elling, "Urbanizing the Iranian Public: Text, Tehran and 1922," *Middle Eastern Studies* 55, no. 3 (2019): 301–318, where he notes that "the novel at once reflected and propelled a crucial shift in cultural frames and forms, which can be termed *the urbanization of the Iranian public*" (301, emphasis in the original).

28. The quote is from Pedersen, *Rise of the Persian Novel*, 141. *Ruzgar-i siyah* (Dark days) was first published in 1924. A second printing digital edition is at http://dl.nlai.ir /UI/048a3750–094e-4996-baab-64c9b8b33a1e/LookInside.aspx. Ramadan 1343, printed by Kitabkhanah-i Kaveh, is a digital copy of the fourth edition published in 1936, http:// dl.nlai.ir/UI/58de8e87-ba90–43b6-ac52-9d400e7f684e/LookInside.aspx. For an English summary of the plot and its discussion, see Pedersen, *Rise of the Persian Novel*, 136 (which translates the title as *Ill Fate*).

29. Mushfiq Kazimi, *Tihran-i makhauf*, 180–181.

30. *Huma* (first published in 1927). The edition that I cited here is the fifth printing, published in 1960 (Tehran: Ibn Sina).

31. Ghanoonparvar, "Ḥejāzi, Moḥammad Moṭiʿ-al-Dawla."

32. Pedersen, *Rise of the Persian Novel*, 175.

33. Murtiza Mushfiq Kazimi, *Yadigar-i yik shab* (Tehran, 1926). The edition that I cited here was published in 1961 (Tehran: Ibn Sina).

34. Mushfiq Kazimi, *Tihran-i makhauf*, 156.

35. Mushfiq Kazimi, *Yadigar-i yik shab*, 57.

36. Mushfiq Kazimi, *Yadigar-i yik shab*, 59.

37. Mushfiq Kazimi, *Yadigar-i yik shab*, 66.

38. Pedersen, *Rise of the Persian Novel*, 175.

39. Sheida Dayani, "Juggling Revolutionaries: A Theatrical History of Indigenous Theatre and Early Playwriting in Iran" (PhD diss., New York University, 2018), 9.

40. Dayani, "Juggling Revolutionaries," 10.

41. See Dayani, "Juggling Revolutionaries," 114–124 (for the first play) and 124–133 (for the second play).

42. For more historical information and discussion of *Mulla Nasr al-Din*, see Muʿin al-Din Mihrabi, "Nigahi beh ruznameh-i *Mulla Nasr al-Din*," *Kitab-i mah*, April/May 2008, 40–47; Evan Siegel, "A Woman's Letters to *Molla Nasr od-Din* (Tiflis)," in *Presse und Öffentlichkeit im Nahen Östen*, ed. Christopher Herzog et al. (Heidelberg: Heidelberg Orientverlag, 1995), 143–153. See also Janet Afary and Kamran Afary, "*Mollā Nasreddin* and the Creative Cauldron of Transcaucasia," *British Journal of Middle Eastern Studies*, 14 September 2019, doi: 10.1080/13530194.2019.1659130. For a selection of articles from *Mulla Nasr al-Din*, translated into Persian, see Farhad Dashtaki-nia, trans., *Sarguzasht-i sayeh-ha: Haftad maqaleh-yi majalleh-yi Mulla Nasr al-Din dar bareh-yi zanan va kudakan* (Tehran: Nashr-i Tarikh-i Iran, 2016).

Three volumes of *Mulla Nasr al-Din* can be accessed at http://www.qajarwomen.org /en/items/15160A3.html. For the problems of a man with four wives, see https://iiif.lib .harvard.edu/manifests/view/drs:424428111$287i.

For other similar issues, see the following links: https://iiif.lib.harvard.edu/manifests /view/drs:424428111$299i; https://iiif.lib.harvard.edu/manifests/view/drs:424428111$307i; https://iiif.lib.harvard.edu/manifests/view/drs:424428111$311i; https://iiif.lib.harvard.edu /manifests/view/drs:424428111$315i; https://iiif.lib.harvard.edu/manifests/view/drs :424428111$327i; https://iiif.lib.harvard.edu/manifests/view/drs:424428111$364i; https:// iiif.lib.harvard.edu/manifests/viewdrs:424428111$374i; https://iiif.lib.harvard.edu/manifests /view/drs:424428111$382i; https://iiif.lib.harvard.edu/manifests/view/drs:424428111 $434i; https://iiif.lib.harvard.edu/manifests/view/drs:424428111$446i; https://iiif.lib.harvard .edu/manifests/view/drs:424428111$470i; https://iiif.lib.harvard.edu/manifests/view/drs :424428111$486i; https://iiif.lib.harvard.edu/manifests/view/drs:424428111$490i; https:// iiif.lib.harvard.edu/manifests/view/drs:424428111$498i; https://iiif.lib.harvard.edu /manifests/view/drs:424428111$508i; https://iiif.lib.harvard.edu/manifests/view/drs :424428111$514i; https://iiif.lib.harvard.edu/manifests/view/drs:424428111$520i; https:// iiif.lib.harvard.edu/manifests/view/drs:424428111$538i; https://iiif.lib.harvard.edu /manifests/view/drs:424428111$551i; and https://iiif.lib.harvard.edu/manifests/view/drs :424428111$552i.

Some fifteen years later, popular Persian-language newspapers, among them *Gul-i zard*, would publish satirical songs, criticizing polygyny through the voice of women. See, for instance, vol. 3, no. 25 (25/5/1339 ah / 4 February 1921): 1–2; 34 (1 Shaʿban 1339 / 10 April 1921): 3; 36 (23 Shaʿban 1339 / 2 May 1921): 4; 41 (4 Shawwal 1339 / 11 June 1921): 4; 42 (11

Shawwal 1339 /18 June 1921): 3; vol. 4, no. 7 (15 /12/1339 / 20 August 1921): 4; 16 (11/3/1340 / 12 November 1921): 4; 20 (1/5/1340 / 31 December 1921): 4; 26 (27 Rajab 1340 / 26 March 1922): 1–2.

43. Sheida Dayani, email communication, 13 March 2019.

44. Bibi Khanum Astarabadi, *Ma'ayib al-rijal* (Vices of men), http://www.qajarwomen .org/en/items/904A5.html, and *Disciplining Women*, http://www.qajarwomen.org/en /items/904A3.html. For further discussion and identification of *Disciplining Women*'s author, see Ruhangiz Karachi, "Who Is the Original Author of Ta'dib al-nisvan?," *Tarikh-i adabiyat* 65, no. 3 (Summer 2010): 199–208. The author of this text is most probably Khanlar Mirza Ihtisham al-Dawlah (d. 1861, a son of Fath 'Ali Shah).

45. *Ma'ayib al-rijal*, 57 (print version, Chicago: Midland Press, 1992).

46. Amy Stanley, "Maidservants' Tales: Narrating Domestic and Global History in Eurasia, 1600–1900," *American Historical Review* 121, no. 2 (2016): 437–460; Taj al-Saltaneh, *Khatirat*, ed. Mansureh Ittihadiyeh and Cirus Sa'dvandiyan (Tehran: Nashr-i Tarikh-i Iran, 1983), 110.

47. "Zhandark" in the school name is for "Jeanne d'Arc." For more about the Tarbiyat school, see Jasamin Rostam-Kolayi, "The *Tarbiyat* Girls' School of Tehran: Iranian and American Baha'i Contributions to Modern Education," *Middle East Critique* 22, no. 1 (2013): 77–93.

48. Mihrmah Farmanfarmayan, *Zir-i nigah-i pidar: Khatirat-i Mihrmah Farmanfar-mayiyan az andaruni* (Tehran: Kavir, 2004), 247.

49. Farmanfarmayan, *Zir-i nigah-i pidar*, 316.

50. Farmanfarmayan, *Zir-i nigah-i pidar*, 334.

51. Bihbihani, *Ba madaram hamrah*, 21–22.

52. Surur al-Saltaneh's father (Muhammad 'Ali Khan Khazin al-Mulk) was a steward of Nayyir al-Mulk (a Qajar prince and governor of Khurasan). After his first wife's death (Surur al-Saltaneh's mother), Khazin al-Mulk had married Nayyir al-Mulk's daughter, Shams al-Saltaneh. Taymurtash's family were large landowners in the Khurasan, Bujnurd, area.

For Surur al-Saltaneh's familial information, see http://www.qajarwomen.org/en /people/1233.html; http://www.qajarwomen.org/en/people/2296.html; and http://www .qajarwomen.org/en/people/2651.html.

53. For these Taymurtash and Surur al-Saltaneh letters, see http://www.qajarwomen .org/en/items/13110A22.html.

54. Affectionate letters we have from the earlier Qajar period include the Qa'im Maqam letters (http://www.qajarwomen.org/en/items/14150A24.html; http://www.qajar women.org/en/items/14150A25.html); the Shaykh al-Islam letters (Sakineh Khanum to her husband, Mirza Hasan Shaykh al-Islam, http://www.qajarwomen.org/en/items/1016A15 .html); Fatimeh Khanum Farah al-Saltaneh's letters, including those to her husband, Mirza Hasan Shaykh al-Islam (http://www.qajarwomen.org/en/items/1016A63.html); letters from Mirza Hasan Shaykh al-Islam to his wife, Rukhsareh Khanum (http://www.qajarwomen .org/en/items/1139A40.html); and letters of Nusrat al-Saltaneh and A'zam al-Saltaneh (http://www.qajarwomen.org/en/items/1023A6.html).

55. On this issue, see also Amin, *Making of the Modern Iranian Woman*.

56. I borrow the expression "sexual monogamy" from Motlagh, *Burying the Beloved*, 65.

57. Zanjani, *Khatirat-i Shaykh Ibrahim Zanjani*, 102.

58. For the marriage to Tatiyana Markariyan, see http://www.qajarwomen.org/en/people/2653.html and http://www.qajarwomen.org/en/items/13110A21.html. I have not been able to find any further information on his third wife. That marriage is reported by American Consul, Charles Hart (U.S. State Department File 891.405/11, 2), as quoted in Amin, *Making of the Modern Iranian Woman*, 135.

59. Among these romance books were *Marie Rose* (ماری رز), *Love and Virtue* (عشق و فضیلت), *Love's Tears* (اشک های عشق), *Samileh* (ثمیله), *Shirin, A Boy's Pain* (رنج پس), and *Mina* (آشیان فراق). See the first volume of Giti Afruz's diaries, written in 1938–1939, when she was thirteen, at http://www.qajarwomen.org/fa/items/1251B78.html.

60. Among the movies Giti mentions in her diaries were *The Fate's Spring* (چشمه تقدیر), *Made for Each Other* (1939, dir. David Selznick, بوسه آتشین), *The Little Princess* (1939, with Shirley Temple), *Suez* (1938, dir. Allan Dwan), and Laurel and Hardy films. Many of the films' identifications I have taken from the versions of Giti Afruz's diaries as transcribed and edited by Samila Amir Ebrahimi. For a fuller list, see the link in note 58.

61. The unpublished third book of Giti's memoirs includes a most valuable list of the films that she and her friends saw in the mid-1940s, especially as annotated by Samila Amir Ebrahimi. *Back Street* (1931) was a best-selling novel by Fannie Hurst. Three film versions were produced, in 1932 (dir. John Stahi), 1941 (dir. Robert Stevenson), and 1961 (dir. David Miller).

62. On sigheh/mut'a, see Shahla Haeri, *Law of Desire: Temporary Marriage in Shi'i Iran* (Syracuse, NY: Syracuse University Press, 1989), and Shahla Haeri, "Mot'a," *Encyclopaedia Iranica*, accessed 12 March 2019, http://www.iranicaonline.org/articles/mota.

63. On the urban middle-class perception of sigheh as legalized prostitution, see Haeri, *Law of Desire*, x, 6, 201, 209.

64. Haeri, "Mot'a." See also Shahla Haeri, "Temporary Marriage: An Islamic Discourse on Female Sexuality in Iran," *Social Research* 59, no. 1 (1992): 201–223.

65. On the issue of men keeping their sigheh wives secret, see Claudia Yaghoobi, *Temporary Marriage in Iran: Gender and Body Politics in Modern Iranian Film and Literature* (Cambridge: Cambridge University Press, 2020), 10, 13.

66. Reported in *Shargh*, 24 September 2014, 14.

67. The genealogy was generated by Manuchihr Najmabadi (completed in the summer of 2001).

68. Khadijeh Afzal Vaziri, transcript of her interview with her son, Husayn'ali Mallah, http://www.qajarwomen.org/en/items/14129A59.html; see the manuscript version, 41, 54, 57, 62.

69. Afzal Vaziri, transcript manuscript, 49, 129.

70. Afzal Vaziri, transcript manuscript, 74.

71. Afzal Vaziri, transcript manuscript, 60.

72. Afzal Vaziri, transcript manuscript, 128–129.

73. Nusrat Zaman and her second husband also socialized extensively with the Mallahs, and Khanum Afzal's children would call her Maman Parvin. Guli was called Khaleh (Aunt) Guli by Mahlaqa's children, one of whom considered her the favorite aunt.

74. Mahlaqa Mallah did not want to marry her first husband, Muhammad Zaman Bayat, a grandson of her mother's aunt, but she was pressured to agree.

75. Interview with Mahlaqa Mallah, June 2014, http://www.qajarwomen.org/en/items /14129A1.html and http://www.qajarwomen.org/en/items/14129A60.html.

76. Narjis Mihrangiz Mallah, *Az zanan-i pishgam-i Irani: Afzal Vaziri, dukhtar-i Bibi Khanum Astarabadi* (Tehran: Shirazeh, 2006), 33–34.

77. Mallah, *Az zanan*, 41.

CHAPTER 2. OBJECTS

1. The Surur al-Saltaneh and 'Abd al-Husayn Taymurtash letters, 1909–1910, are at http://www.qajarwomen.org/en/items/13110A22.html. For the letters of Shams al-Muluk 'Azudi and her husband, Hisam al-Dawlah, 1913–1914, see http://www.qajarwomen.org /en/items/1134A3.html and http://www.qajarwomen.org/en/items/1134D14.html. For letters between A'zam al-Saltaneh and Nusrat al-Saltaneh, see http://www.qajarwomen.org /en/items/1023A6.html. Letters of Mahdiquli Mirza Nusrat Muzaffari are at http://www .qajarwomen.org/en/items/1023A103.html. For the letters of Badr al-Muluk and Amin al-Sultan, and other unidentified writers and receivers, see http://www.qajarwomen.org/en /items/1282A2.html; http://www.qajarwomen.org/en/items/1282A4.html; and http:// www.qajarwomen.org/en/items/1282A13.html.

2. Farrukh Ghaffari, ed., *Mahin Banu* (Tehran: Farzan, 2001), 39.

3. This passage is in http://www.qajarwomen.org/en/items/1023A6.html, seq. 23.

4. This passage is in http://www.qajarwomen.org/en/items/1023A6.html, seq. 50.

5. Beth Baron points this out as well in "The Making and Breaking of Marital Bonds in Modern Egypt," in *Women in Middle Eastern History: Shifting Boundaries in Sex and Gender*, ed. Nikki R. Keddie and Beth Baron (New Haven, CT: Yale University Press, 1991), 275–291.

6. At one point, he had been pressured into marrying Fakhr al-Saltaneh, a daughter of Nizam al-Saltaneh Mafi, but he never consummated that marriage and eventually divorced her (she subsequently married Shaykh Khaz'al).

7. Baqir 'Aqili, ed., *Khatirat-i Haj 'Izz al-Mamalik Ardalan* (Tehran: Namak, 1993), 11. Unfortunately, from the ten volumes of his handwritten memoirs, over 1,000 pages, a selection of material has been published, in which the editor "deleted what was related to personal and family matters since such matters would not have been of interest to readers" (7).

8. For this envelope, see https://iiif.lib.harvard.edu/manifests/view/drs:37863227$4i, seq. 4.

9. Surur al-Saltaneh's father (Muhammad 'Ali Khan Khazin al-Mulk) was a steward of Nayyir al-Mulk's (a Qajar prince and governor of Khurasan). Her mother, Zarrin Kulah Khanum, was distantly related to the Nayyir al-Mulk family. Surur al-Saltaneh lost her mother in early childhood and her father's second wife was Nayyir al-Mulk's daughter, Shams al-Saltaneh. Her father's marriage to a Qajar princess had further moved up their social location. Taymurtash's family were large landowners in the Khurasan, Bujnurd area. His landowning family may have been well off, but not of the Qajars.

10. Dena Goodman, "Letter Writing and the Emergence of Gendered Subjectivity in Eighteenth-Century France," *Journal of Women's History* 17, no. 2 (Summer 2005): 9–37, quote from 22.

11. These quotes are from the letters of 5 May 1942 and 25 May 1942.

12. Alan Bray writes in *The Friend* (Chicago: University of Chicago Press, 2003) about "hand-writing as a bodily token," emphasizing that letters bearing such bodily tokens could connect bodies that sought passionate togetherness (161–164).

13. Alan Duben and Cem Behar, *Istanbul Households: Marriage, Family and Fertility, 1880–1940* (Cambridge: Cambridge University Press, 1991), 206.

14. Siegfried Kracauer, "Photography," trans. Thomas Y. Levin, *Critical Inquiry* 19 (Spring 1993): 421–436, quote from 422.

15. Bruno Latour, *We Have Never Been Modern* (Cambridge, MA: Harvard University Press, 1993).

16. Svetlana Boym, *The Future of Nostalgia* (New York: Basic Books, 2001).

17. For similar types of bridal wear, see, as well, the following links (all undated): http://www.qajarwomen.org/en/items/1025A195.html; http://www.qajarwomen.org/en/items/1025A143.html; and http://www.qajarwomen.org/en/items/1025A172.html.

18. Sohelia Shahshahani, *Persian Clothing during the Qajar Reign* [book in Persian; English-language title cited here from a translation on the back cover of the book] (Tehran: Farhangsara-yi Mirdashti, 2008), 148. I do not have much information about wedding outfits in other cases.

19. Qahriman Mirza 'Ayn al-Saltaneh Salur, *Ruznamah-'i khatirat-i 'Ayn al-Saltaneh*, 10 vols., ed. Iraj Afshar and Mas'ud Salur (Tehran: Intisharat-i Asatir , 1995–2001), 6:4896.

20. Mihrmah Farmanfarmayan, *Zir-i nigah-i pidar: Khatirat-i Mihrmah Farmanfar-mayiyan az andaruni* (Tehran: Kavir, 2004), 280, 330.

21. Kenneth Cuno, *Modernizing Marriage: Family, Ideology, and Law in Nineteenth- and Early Twentieth-Century Egypt* (Syracuse, NY: Syracuse University Press, 2015), 55.

22. In connection with the significance of domestic objects in general and photographs in particular for shaping the meaning of domesticity and home, see Toufoul Abou-Hodeib, *A Taste for Home: The Modern Middle Class in Ottoman Beirut* (Stanford, CA: Stanford University Press, 2017), especially chapter 4.

23. Beth Baron, *Egypt as a Woman: Nationalism, Gender, and Politics* (Berkeley: University of California Press, 2005); Stephen Sheehi, *The Arab Imago: A Social History of Portrait Photography, 1860–1910* (Princeton, NJ: Princeton University Press, 2016); David J. Roxburgh and Mary McWilliams, eds., *Technologies of the Image: Art in 19th-Century Iran* (Cambridge, MA: Harvard Art Museums, 2017); Zeynep Çelik and Edhem Eldem, eds., *Camera Ottomana: Photography and Modernity in the Ottoman Empire, 1840–1914* (Istanbul: Koç University Publications, 2015); Carmen Pérez González, *Local Portraiture: Through the Lens of the 19th Century Iranian Photographers* (Leiden: Leiden University Press, 2012). For a brilliant analysis of the significance of photography's generative effects in changes of gender and sexual concepts in Iran, see Staci Gem Scheiwiller, *Liminalities of Gender and Sexuality in Nineteenth-Century Iranian Photography: Desirous Bodies* (New York: Routledge, 2017). See also her article "Modern Family: The Transformation of the

Family Photograph in Qajar Iran," *Family Photographs* 9, no. 1 (Fall 2018): http://hdl.handle
.net/2027/spo.7977573.0009.109.

24. Sherry Turkle, ed., *Evocative Objects: Things We Think With* (Cambridge, MA:
MIT Press, 2007), 5.

25. G. Arunima, "Bonds of Love, Ties of Kinship? Or Are There Other Ways of Imagining the Family?," *Indian Economic and Social History Review* 53, no. 3 (2016): 1–22, quote
from 14.

26. Annette Kuhn, *Family Secrets: Acts of Memory and Imagination* (1995; London:
Verso, 2002).

27. Janet Hoskins, *Biographical Objects: How Things Tell the Stories of People's Lives*
(New York: Routledge, 1998). For Laurel Ulrich's latest book, see *A House Full of Females:
Plural Marriage and Women's Rights in Early Mormonism, 1835–1870* (New York: Alfred
A. Knopf, 2017).

28. Hoskins, *Biographical Objects*, 2.

29. See Meir Wigoder, "History Begins at Home: Photography and Memory in the
Writings of Siegfried Kracauer and Roland Barthes," accessed 8 August 2018, https://www
.nyu.edu/classes/bkg/methods/wigoder.pdf; Kracauer, "Photography."

30. Sharon Marcus, *Between Women: Friendship, Desire, and Marriage in Victorian England* (Princeton, NJ: Princeton University Press, 2007).

31. Marianne Hirsch, ed., *The Familial Gaze* (Hanover, NH: University Press of New
England, 1999), xvi.

32. Malek Alloula, *The Colonial Harem*, trans. Myrna Godzich and Wlad Godzich
(Minneapolis: University of Minnesota Press, 1986), 38.

33. See http://search.qajarwomen.com/search?lang=en&filter=genres_en:photographs
|subjects_en:husband%2Band%2Bwife.

34. See also Marianne Hirsch, *Family Frames: Photography, Narrative, and Postmemory*
(Cambridge, MA: Harvard University Press, 1997): "The family photo both displays the
cohesion of the family and is an instrument of its togetherness; it both chronicles family
rituals and constitutes a prime objective of those rituals. Because the photograph gives the
illusion of being a simple transcription of the real, a trace touched directly by the event it
records, it has the effect of naturalizing cultural practices and of disguising their stereo-
typed and coded characteristics" (7).

35. Narjis Mihrangiz Mallah, *Az zanan-i pishgam-i Irani: Afzal Vaziri, dukhtar-i Bibi
Khanum Astarabadi* (Tehran: Shirazeh, 2006).

36. Taped interviews are on the WWQI site. See http://www.qajarwomen.org/en/items
/14129A1.html and http://www.qajarwomen.org/en/items/14129A60.html. For other
Mallah family photographs, visit http://www.qajarwomen.org/en/collections/14129.html.

37. Mushfiq Kazimi, for instance, expressed dismay that his wife would make decisions
over her paternal inheritance in consultation with her mother without seeking his advice,
and he transferred her share to her mother. Murtiza Mushfiq Kazimi, *Ruzgar va andishah-ha*, 2 vols. (Tehran: Ibn Sina, 1973).

1. I discuss these domains more fully in *Women with Mustaches and Men without Beards: Gender and Sexual Anxieties of Iranian Modernity* (Berkeley: University of California Press, 2005), 157–159.

2. On different objectives of nikah and mut'a, see Shahla Haeri, *Law of Desire: Temporary Marriage in Shi'i Iran* (Syracuse, NY: Syracuse University Press, 1989), 50.

3. For examples of dictionaries, see http://www.tyndalearchive.com/tabs/lane/ and https://archive.org/details/cu31924026873194.

4. Naomi Tadmor, "The Concept of the Household-Family in Eighteenth-Century England," *Past and Present* 151 (May 1996): 111–140. She further expands: "Turner's concept of his family is best understood in institutional and instrumental rather than in sentimental terms" (124). That is, some had contractual bonds, as an indentured apprentice, and so on, while others had a service contract or a boarding contract (123). Also, "many of the household-family relationships were both domestic and occupational" (124–125). "Both show how contractual, instrumental and occupational household-family relationships were also entwined with networks of patronage and kinship, in the case of Hannah Marchant extending vertically from the middling household-family to the level of the village poor" (125). "One phrase that recurs in the context of such changes is 'to be taken into the family'" (119).

5. Tadmor, "Concept of the Household-Family," 112–113.

6. Muhammad 'Ali Furughi, *Yaddashtha-yi ruzaneh*, ed. Iraj Afshar (Tehran: Kitabkhaneh, Muzeh va Markaz-i Asnad-i Majlis-i Shawra-yi Islami, 2009), 216, 390.

7. I have not succeeded in identifying a real person of that name who could correspond to this personage and this time period. 'Abbas was close friends with Karim Sa'i from his days at the School of Agriculture and collaborated with him on initiating and planting what was initially called Sa'i Forest, now renamed Sa'i Park. Karim Sa'i's father's name was indeed 'Ali Akbar, but he was a resident of Mashhad. The window of time recorded in the diary would not correspond to 'Ali Akbar's youth, and not much is known about his life to enable me to attribute the booklet to him.

8. See http://www.qajarwomen.org/en/items/1014E1.html.

9. See Sadiqeh Dawlatabadi, *Nameh-ha, nivishteh-ha, and yadha*, ed. Mahdokht Sanati and Afsaneh Najmabadi, 3 vols. (Chicago: Midland Press, 1998), 1:247–253.

10. Murtiza Mushfiq Kazimi, *Ruzgar va andishah-ha*, 2 vols. (Tehran: Ibn Sina, 1973), 1:290–291. It seems that in the 1930s, some urban upper-class men began to socialize in clubs (such as Bashgah-i Iran, or Iran-i javan) or go to hotels that had musical concerts or theatrical performances in the evenings. Mushfiq Kazimi states that he himself often spent his evenings in these clubs (1:306). He also notes that some of these men came to these clubs or hotels with their European or non-Muslim wives. Among them, he notes Davar (the minister of justice) who would come "with his new wife" (1:300; she was presumably more Europeanized than his first more traditional wife) and Taymurtash who would come "with his Armenian wife" (1:307).

11. Qahriman Mirza 'Ayn al-Saltaneh Salur, *Ruznamah-'i khatirat-i 'Ayn al-Saltaneh*, ed. Iraj Afshar and Mas'ud Salur, 10 vols. (Tehran: Intisharat-i Asatir, 1995–2001),

10:7700–7701. He also notes that Taymurtash's "princely wife was a chaste and pious woman."

12. Baqir 'Aqili, ed., *Khatirat-i Haj 'Izz al-Mamalik Ardalan* (Tehran: Namak, 1993): "When I turned fifteen lunar years of age, my parents insisted that they ought to get me a wife.... First, they insisted on getting me a girl as a sigheh; fortunately, this was not consummated; it remained a sigheh in name only, until my maternal cousin was engaged for me" (10). He was born in 1883, so this would have been around 1897–1898. The cousin marriage fell through as well; he was eventually married to Nuzhat al-Dawleh, a granddaughter of Nasir al-Din Shah's, in 1901.

13. Mushfiq Kazimi, *Ruzgar va andishah-ha*, 1:56.

14. For a copy of Kaukab Dargahi and 'Ayn al-Saltaneh's marriage contract, see http://www.qajarwomen.org/fa/items/1140A16.html.

15. All information on his marriages, unless otherwise stated, are from his memoirs, *Ruznamah-'i khatirat-i 'Ayn al-Saltaneh*: 3:1785–1787, 2011, 2275; 4:2872, 2954–2955; 5:3356–3357, 3756, 3757, 3783–3784, 3795, 3856.

16. 'Ayn al-Saltaneh, *Ruznamah-'i khatirat-i 'Ayn al-Saltaneh*, 5:3795.

17. 'Ayn al-Saltaneh, *Ruznamah-'i khatirat-i 'Ayn al-Saltaneh*, 5:3817.

18. 'Ayn al-Saltaneh, *Ruznamah-'i khatirat-i 'Ayn al-Saltaneh*, 10:7832–7833.

19. Lisa Tran notes a similar tendency for twentieth-century China: "The persistence of the stereotype of concubines as victims stems from two ideas implicit in most past studies: 1) the concubine's marginal position in her master's family and 2) the assumed relationship between a woman's agency and her kinship status. Much of past scholarship had tended to interpret the ambiguity of a concubine's relationship to her master's family as her exclusion from kinship structures.... Since only a main wife could be a mother-in-law and grandmother in the eyes of law and society, a concubine found herself effectively excluded from the higher ranks of the female hierarchy." Lisa Tran, *Concubines in Court: Marriage and Monogamy in Twentieth-Century China* (Lanham, MD: Rowman and Littlefield, 2015), 5. Her observations of why a wife would agree and even select a concubine for her husband echo similar reports on Iran, as we have seen: "Given that marriages were arranged, concubinage offered a husband dissatisfied with his parents' choice the possibility to choose for himself a woman who better suited his preferences. For the wife, too, a concubine could be a welcome addition to the household as she could hand over to the concubine those tasks she disliked" (9).

20. See Shahla Haeri, "Mot'a," *Encyclopaedia Iranica*, accessed 12 March 2019, http://www.iranicaonline.org/articles/mota.

21. Patience turned out to be the quality many relatives recalled over and over again when talking about Fari herself; she was a very patient woman, including in her married life; she faced troubles patiently (*ba-sabr*), from dealing with challenges of living with her mother-in-law to coping with 'Abbas's possible affairs and then the knowledge of another wife.

22. Simin Bihbihani, *Ba madaram hamrah: Zindigi-namah-'i khudnivisht* (Tehran: Sukhan, 2011), 53.

23. Mihrmah Farmanfarmayan, *Zir-i nigah-i pidar: Khatirat-i Mihrmah Farmanfarmayiyan az andaruni* (Tehran: Kavir, 2004), 203.

24. Such was the case with the Dawlatabadi family. Sadiqeh Dawlatabadi (1882/1883–1961) was married to I'tizad al-Hukama' (later known as Dr. I'tizad) at the age of twenty. In 1921, she used a power of attorney that her father had included in her marriage contract to get divorced from him. Her two younger paternal sisters, Fakhr Taj (1907–1983) and Qamar Taj (1908–1992), similarly married and divorced several times. The Dawlatabadi women developed a reputation for "being prone to ask for divorce" into the next generation.

25. Bihbihani, *Ba madaram hamrah*, 51–53.

26. Bihbihani, *Ba madaram hamrah*, 50.

27. Bihbihani, *Ba madaram hamrah*, 337–339.

28. The incident also clarified an issue that had remained a mystery until then. When Khanum jun's youngest son was born, she wanted to name him Hasan. Shaykh 'Abbas would not hear of it, without giving any explanation for his vehement opposition (that he already had another son with the same name). Eventually, they compromised and named the son Abu al-Hasan.

29. Bibi Khanum Astarabadi, *Ma'ayib al-rijal* (Vices of men), http://www.qajarwomen .org/en/items/904A5.html, 89–90 (my translation).

30. In this connection, see Mostafa Abedinifard, "Persian 'Rashti Jokes': Modern Iran's Palimpsests of *Gheyrat*-Based Masculinity," *British Journal of Middle Eastern Studies*, 22 March 2018, doi: 10.1080/13530194.2018.1447440.

31. Astarabadi, *Ma'ayib al-rijal*, 91.

32. Astarabadi, *Ma'ayib al-rijal*, 91–93.

33. See http://www.qajarwomen.org/en/items/14129A59.html.

34. Maryam was married first to the famous male singer Ghulamhusayn Banan. They had one daughter, Giti. She later married Mr. Zargar; they had one son (Umid) and one daughter (Taraneh).

35. In a later letter, dated 11 March 1995, Mihrangiz elaborated, "I was happy that [our relative—name withheld] had mentioned Khaleh [Aunt] Maryam and I laughed, because the moon doesn't stay covered by clouds forever [that is, the truth comes out]. I will tell you the reason for which I had not mentioned her name in my mother's book. When several years after my mother's death my late brother Husayn'ali gave me the tapes to transcribe, I too was surprised that my mother had not mentioned Maryam's name. Same with not mentioning Guli. When we were in Tehran for five years, my father [then living in Mazandaran] had married Guli's mother, Guli was born, her mother was divorced, my father joined us in Tehran. My mother had never displayed the slightest disrespect toward Maryam or Guli." She goes on to offer several possible reasons for these absences in her mother's text, ending with "I reflected on these issues and respecting her wishes, I wrote the text as she would have wanted it." Sensing that this may not be a topic she would want to further elaborate on, I did not pursue it.

36. For interviews with Mahlaqa Mallah, see http://www.qajarwomen.org/en/items /14129A1.html and http://www.qajarwomen.org/en/items/14129A60.html.

37. Khadijeh Afzal Vaziri, transcript of her interview with her son, Husayn'ali Mallah, http://www.qajarwomen.org/en/items/14129A59.html; see the manuscript version, p. 17, note 3, for *nizamnameh*, and p. 122 for *kitabnameh*.

38. Bibi Khanum's older daughter, Mawlud A'lam al-Saltaneh, continued her mother's work, opening a new school, Parvarish-i dushizigan (which meant "girls' upbringing"). Reported in *Iran-i naw*, 26 July 1911.

39. Afzal Vaziri, transcript manuscript, 13. According to Afzal Vaziri, Bibi Khanum had moved the school to a new rented location (12), rather than moving her husband and grown-up sons. This is less likely because Bibi Khanum later transferred the ownership of her (owned) house to Afzal Vaziri. She died four years before Musa Khan, who continued to live in the other (rental) residence.

40. See the photograph at http://www.qajarwomen.org/en/items/14129A47.html. For other examples, see http://www.qajarwomen.org/en/items/14129A43.html; http://www.qajarwomen.org/en/items/14129A37.html; http://www.qajarwomen.org/en/items/14129A36.html (Giti, her daughter, is also in this photograph); and http://www.qajarwomen.org/en/items/14129A53.html.

41. Astarabadi, *Ma'ayib al-rijal*, 132, note 83.

42. See the letters of 10 March 1996 and 13 April 1996, in specific reference to her uncles and, in more general terms, "in our family."

43. Many of these transactions are recorded in the books of registry of Shaykh Mahdi Najmabadi and Shaykh Baqir Najmabadi. See http://www.qajarwomen.org/en/items/1014B11.html and http://www.qajarwomen.org/en/items/1014C24.html, entry numbers 1855, 1869, 2229, 2563, 6969, 9531, and 9222.

44. *Khatirat-i Haj 'Izz al-Mamalik Ardalan*, 7, mentions that Muzaffar al-Din Shah's courtiers who came with him from Tabriz had, for a while, replaced previous courtiers. His father, for instance, was one of the "paper readers" for Nasir al-Din Shah. See p. 9 for the discussion of the new king Vakil al-Mulk Diba and Vakil al-Dawleh as his paper readers.

45. This was much the same way as, years later, I learned music reading. Only once I had already learned a piece by heart from my *santur* teacher could I read the musical notes to play back. To this day, I cannot read music the other way around.

46. Ironically, this also meant that she had no literacy skills. At this time, girls either went to Qur'anic *maktabs* or, in some families, would be tutored at home.

47. The confirmation of inheritance and list of inheritors are registered in Shaykh Muhammad Taqi Najmabadi's registry, vol. 9, record number 16492; see http://www.qajarwomen.org/en/items/14128A26.html.

48. One famous large and complex household was that of Farmanfarma. The Farmanfarma complex in Tehran is described in Sattareh Farman Farmaian's book *Daughter of Persia: A Woman's Journey from Her Father's Harem through the Islamic Revolution* (London: Bantam Press, 1992) (in at least the first five chapters), by Mihrmah Farmanfarmayan, and in Shahroukh Firouz's book, *Dar Sayeh-i Alburz* [Under the shade of Alborz: A memoir] (Odenton, MD: Mage Persian Editions, 2011), which also has a sketch.

49. The birth certificate for Ziya' is at http://www.qajarwomen.org/en/items/1391A26.html.

1. Judith Goldstein, "Iranian Jewish Women's Magical Narratives," in *Discourse and the Social Life of Meaning*, ed. June R. Wyman (Washington, DC: Smithsonian Institution Press, 1986), 147–168, quote from 162.

2. Ashkan Rezvani-Naraghi, "Middle Class Urbanism: The Socio-spatial Transformation of Tehran, 1921–41," *Iranian Studies* 51, no. 1 (2018): 97–126, quote from 99.

3. Georg Simmel, "Secrecy," in *Sociology of Georg Simmel*, ed. and trans. Kurt H. Wolff (New York: Free Press, 1967), 330–344, quotes are from 330.

4. Simmel, "Secrecy," 330, note 3. The secret, again to quote Simmel, "creates the tempting challenge to break through it, by gossip or confession—and this challenge accompanies its psychology like a constant overtone. The sociological significance of the secret, therefore, has its practical extent, its mode of realization, only in the individual's capacity or inclination to keep it to himself, in his resistance or weakness in the face of tempting betrayal" (334). In 'Abbas's case, he was not tempted to confess to the end of his life: he made sure there was no possibility of gossip, and, remarkably, his other family respected his wish for secrecy to his death.

5. Simin Bihbihani, *Ba madaram hamrah: Zindigi-namah-'i khudnivisht* (Tehran: Sukhan, 2011), 47.

6. There is a vast literature, both in Persian and in English (and most likely in other languages), on the transformation of Tehran over the past centuries, in particular from the late Qajar period, through the Pahlavis, and to the present day. For the purpose of the arguments in this chapter, I have found several sources particularly helpful. Mina Marefat's work remains critical: "Building to Power: Architecture of Tehran 1921–1941" (PhD diss., MIT, 1988), https://dspace.mit.edu/handle/1721.1/14535. In this dissertation, in particular, see pp. 52–66 on mahallas (neighborhoods) of Tehran, pp. 77–79 on the destruction of Sangilaj as a mahalla, and pp. 153–188 for "Part III: Private Architecture: The Construction of Values." 'Abd Allah Anvar's series of essays, first published in several volumes of *Kitab-i Tihran* in the 1990s by Rawshangaran, appeared in several issues of the journal *Payab* from 2010 to 2012. Muhsin Mu'tamidi, *Jughrafiya-yi tarikhi-i Tihran* (Tehran: Markaz-i Nashr-i Danishgahi, 2002); Pamela Karimi, *Domesticity and Consumer Culture in Iran: Interior Revolutions of the Modern Era* (New York: Routledge, 2013).

7. See, in particular, Qahriman Mirza 'Ayn al-Saltaneh Salur, *Ruznamah-'i khatirat-i 'Ayn al-Saltaneh*, 10 vols. (Tehran: Intisharat-i Asatir, 1995–2001), 1:269–270, 273–274, 352–353, 522, 577, 707, 889, 716, 905. In later volumes, he records the presence of women in other places, and not only on specific days, as we shortly will see.

8. Ali Gheissari, "*Khatt va Rabt*: The Significance of Private Papers for Qajar Historiography," Gingko Library, News Blog, originally posted on 5 August 2015, last accessed 26 March 2019, https://www.gingko.org.uk/essays/khatt-va-rabt-significance-private -papers-qajar-historiography/.

9. These schools were Iftitahiyeh, 'Ilmiyieh (both in 1897), Khirad, Muzaffari, Adab, Sadat, Sharaf (all in 1898), Muzaffari School of Agronomy (Filahat—later transformed into Karaj College of Agriculture—1899), 'Ulum-i Siyasi (Political Science, 1899), Kamaliyeh (1899), Islam, and Qudsiyeh (both before 1902). See David Menashri, "Education xvii.

Higher Education," *Encyclopaedia Iranica*, accessed 24 June 2021, https://iranicaonline.org/articles/education-xvii-higher-education.

10. See Marefat, "Building to Power." A particular section of interest is pp. 81–94 on the emergence of khiyaban (no longer simply a passageway, ma'bar) as an urban organizing grid. Mihrmah Farmanfarmayan and Shahroukh Firouz in their memoirs describe at length the structure of the large Farmanfarma household, including the dead-end around which many of them lived; this dead-end was also experienced simply as a ma'bar, a passage that made going from one house to the other part of their childhood movements.

11. On Laleh-zar, Amiriyeh, and other major khiyabans of this period, see Mohsen Motamedi, *Jughrafiya-yi tarikhi-i Tihran* (Tehran: Markaz-i Nashr-i Danishgahi, 2002).

12. Muhammad 'Ali Furughi, *Yaddashtha-yi ruzaneh*, ed. Iraj Afshar (Tehran: Kitab-khaneh, Muzeh va Markaz-i Asnad-i Majlis-i Shawra-yi Islami, 2009).

13. These schools included Siyasi, 'Ilmiyeh, Khirad, Adab, Kamaliyeh, Aliyans (Alliance), and, for a while, Muzaffari.

14. See also Afshin Marashi, "Print Culture and Its Publics: A Social History of Bookstores in Tehran, 1900–1950," *International Journal of Middle East Studies* 47 (2015): 89–108. He quotes Sa'id Nafisi's memoirs, which includes a similar description: "Beneath the Shams al-'Imara, at the end of Nasir Khusraw Street, Shaykh Hasan Kitabfurush owned the most famous bookstore of that time. . . . It was common that each day from sometime in the afternoon until the beginning of nightfall, those who were interested in learning would gather in this bookstore. . . . With Shaykh Hasan, who was a learned man, they would sit on the benches that had been placed along both sides of the shop . . . discuss a wide range of topics . . . and bring tea from the nearby coffeehouse" (89).

15. See also Sa'id Nafisi, *Khatirat-i adabi, siyasi, va javani*, ed. 'Aliriza I'tisami (Tehran: Nashr-i Markaz, 2002), 541–543, for places of leisure strolling of his time, and 611–616 about the structure of his paternal house. Also see Murtiza Mushfiq Kazimi, *Ruzgar va andishah-ha*, 2 vols. (Tehran: Ibn Sina, 1973), 1:123–134, about his circle of young male friends and their hangouts and hobbies, including their daily *gardish* (literally going around—strolling outdoors) in Laleh-zar. Rezvani-Naraghi, in several sections of his article, "Middle Class Urbanism," excellently covers the changing spaces of communal life and urban socialization. In his article, see "From Coffeehouses to Cafés" (7–12), "From Takiyyehs and Religious Performances to Cinemas and Theaters" (12–16), and "From Zurkhanehs to Sport Clubs" (16–18). See also figure 3 in the article, which shows the "distribution of modern social spaces in Tehran 1949" according to different types and their density in old Tehran and in its expanded areas.

16. Among these streets and areas were Laleh-zar, Amiriyeh, Qulhak, Zargandeh, Darband, and Tajrish.

17. For the alarming tone in which women's public mixing with men is recorded in some memoirs, even as the writer notes his and his friends' voyeuristic pleasures, see 'Ayn al-Saltaneh, *Ruznamah-'i khatirat-i*, 8:6442, 6486, 6494–6495, 6642; 9:7065, 7087, 7126, 7154, 7158, 7279.

18. See, for instance, Dust'alikhan Mu'ayyir al-Mamalik, *Vaqayi' al-zaman: Khatirat-i shikariyah*, ed. Khadijeh Nizam Mafi (Tehran: Nashr-i Tarikh-i Iran, 1982), for several 1911 entries, on 30–31, 38–39, 50, 58, 70.

19. See, for instance, *Shukufah*, 1:14, 31 August 1913 (p. 13); 1:15, 21 September 1913 (p. 3); 2:8, 17 March 1914 (pp. 3–4); 2:19, 27 September 1914 (pp. 3–4). Numerous articles in *Gul-i zard* and other journals harped on the same concerns.

20. For Nasim-i Shumal, see *Kulliyat-i javdanah Nasim-i Shumal*, ed. Husayn Namini (Tehran: Asatir, 1992), 775–781.

21. On Laleh-zar, see also Ja'far Shahri, *Tihran-i qadim*, vol. 1 (Tehran: Mu'in, 1991), 276–284.

22. See 'Ayn al-Saltaneh, *Ruznamah-'i khatirat-i*, 5:3811. See also Hamid Naficy, *A Social History of Iranian Cinema*, vol. 1: *The Artisanal Era, 1897–1941* (Durham, NC: Duke University Press, 2011), 130–132, and also the following sections of this latter book: "Modern Streets, Flâneurs, and Moviegoing"; chapter 5, "Modernity's Ambivalent Subjectivity: Dandies and the Dandy Movie Genre."

23. For a detailed description, see Farrukh Ghaffari, ed., *Mahin Banu* (Tehran: Farzan, 2001), 253–257.

24. The strategy of selling the properties around Hasanabad Maydan coincidentally served the family well, as within a decade, with the rise of Riza Shah to power, large household complexes in central Tehran were taken over for state use. For the takeover of the Farmanfarma complex of houses, see Shahroukh Firouz, *Dar Sayeh-i Alburz* [Under the shade of Alborz: A memoir; this is the English title as on the back cover] (Odenton, MD: Mage Persian Editions, 2011), 4 (for the plan of the complex before the takeover), 12 (for the plan during the Pahlavi period); see also pp. 199–202. See also Ghaffari, *Mahin Banu*, 167: "The larger half of Mansuriyeh [her father's complex] was taken over by Madrasah-i Nizam, the later Danishkadeh-i Afsari [Military Academy]."

25. Conversation with author.

26. See documents with registry numbers 9531 and 12102 at https://iiif.lib.harvard.edu /manifests/view/drs:16067660$832i and https://iiif.lib.harvard.edu/manifests/view /drs:16067660$1047i.

27. Minoo Javan's site is http://www.minoojavan.com/.

28. See Mytheli Sreenivas, *Wives, Widows, Concubines: The Conjugal Family Ideal in Colonial India* (Bloomington: Indiana University Press, 2008). In particular, pp. 21–41 discuss varying modes of incorporation into households in India that at times recall similarities with Iran.

29. The generated sense of intimate kinship between them had been such a strong family impression that when I reconnected with Turan, then living in Tennessee, decades later in the spring of 2015, it was one of the first things she mentioned: "the funny perception that I had married my uncle." She repeated it later with a laugh, "I am both your cousin and your uncle's wife!"

30. Several times when she had called me and I wasn't home, her message on the answering machine would start, "This is Turan, your cousin, Gawhar al-Muluk's daughter." She would never say, "This is your uncle's wife, Turan," as if an identification through a marital affiliation was more distant than through "fictive cousinhood." I generally do not use "fictive kin," since in an important sense all kin is fictive; put another way, I am never certain what would constitute fictive versus what.

31. For the Tarbiyat schools, see Soli Shahvar, *The Forgotten Schools: The Baha'is and*

Modern Education in Iran, 1899–1934 (London: I. B. Tauris, 2009), 157–158. For a series of vignettes about life in the old Bazarcheh Aqa Shaykh Hadi, in the Amiriyeh neighborhood, see https://www.facebook.com/pg/Amirieh-%D8%A7%D9%85%DB%8C %D8%B1%DB%8C%D9%87–208939239175174/photos/?tab=album&album_id =674175505984876.

EPILOGUE

1. In marriage contracts, however, a contract between two individuals, *nakih* and *mankuhah*, *zauj* and *zaujah*, were and are used to refer to the groom and the bride.

2. Mihrmah Farmanfarmayan, *Zir-i nigah-i pidar: Khatirat-i Mihrmah Farmanfarmay-iyan az andaruni* (Tehran: Kavir, 2004), 43, 44.

3. Farmanfarmayan, *Zir-i nigah-i pidar*, 60.

4. Farrukh Ghaffari, ed., *Mahin Banu* (Tehran: Farzan, 2001), 21.

5. Qahriman Mirza ʿAyn al-Saltaneh Salur, *Ruznamah-ʾi khatirat-i ʿAyn al-Saltaneh*, 10 vols. (Tehran: Intisharat-i Asatir, 1995–2001), 10:7624.

6. ʿAyn al-Saltaneh, *Ruznamah-ʾi khatirat-i ʿAyn al-Saltaneh*, 3:2287.

7. Nazila Nazimi, ed., *Sih ruz bih akhar-i darya: Safarnamah-i shahzadah khanum-i Qajari* (Tehran: Atraf, 2018), 23.

8. "They are contracting a marriage between the daughter of Hishmat al-Dawlah's wife, who is the daughter of brother of Nasir al-Saltanah and Saʿid al-Saltanah, for Nasir al-Saltanah's son, Muhtahsim al-Saltanah." Muhsin Mirzaʾi, ed., *Ruznamah-i khatirat-i Ghu-lamʿali Khan ʿAziz al-Sultan*, 4 vols. (Tehran: Zaryab, 1997), 3:2256.

9. ʿAyn al-Saltaneh, *Ruznamah-ʾi khatirat-i ʿAyn al-Saltaneh*, 1:45.

10. Murtiza Mushfiq Kazimi, *Tihran-i makhauf*, 5th ed. (Tehran: Ibn Sina, 1961), 55.

11. The Munis Aqa story is based on Mahdokht Sanati's introduction in Sadiqeh Daw-latabadi, *Nameh-ha, nivishteh-ha, and yadha*, ed. Mahdokht Sanati and Afsaneh Naj-mabadi, 3 vols. (Chicago: Midland Press, 1998); Zohreh Sullivan, *Exiled Memories: Stories of Iranian Diaspora* (Philadelphia: Temple University Press, 2001); and several conversations with Mahdokht Sanati.

12. Shaykh Ibrahim Zanjani, *Khatirat-i Shaykh Ibrahim Zanjani: Sarʾguzasht-i zinda-gani-i man*, ed. Ghulamhusayn Mirza (Tehran: Kavir, 2001), 157.

13. See Afzal Vaziri's memoir, https://iiif.lib.harvard.edu/manifests/view/drs :424427393$89i, p. 86, and printed version (1996, p. 39; 2006, p. 60).

14. Several conversations, and an email of 16 October 2014, with Nasrin Abolhasani.

15. Ghaffari, *Mahin Banu*, 153, 172, 218. See also Simin Bihbihani, *Ba madaram ham-rah: Zindigi-namah-ʾi khudnivisht* (Tehran: Sukhan, 2011), 173, where she does use "na-pidari" (stepfather).

Abedinifard, Mostafa. "Persian 'Rashti Jokes': Modern Iran's Palimpsests of *Gheyrat-Based Masculinity." *British Journal of Middle Eastern Studies*, 22 March 2018. doi: 10.1080/13530194.2018.1447440.

Abou-Hodeib, Toufoul. *A Taste for Home: The Modern Middle Class in Ottoman Beirut.* Stanford, CA: Stanford University Press, 2017.

Abu-Lughod, Lila, ed. *Remaking Women: Feminism and Modernity in the Middle East.* Princeton, NJ: Princeton University Press, 1998.

Abu-Lughod, Lila. *Writing Women's Worlds.* Berkeley: University of California Press, 1993.

Afary, Janet, and Kamran Afary. "*Mollā Nasreddin* and the Creative Cauldron of Transcaucasia." *British Journal of Middle Eastern Studies*, 14 September 2019. doi: 10.1080/13530194.2019.1659130.

Afzal Vaziri, Khadijeh. Transcript of her interview with her son, Husayn'ali Mallah. Accessed 17 May 2021. http://www.qajarwomen.org/en/items/14129A59.html.

Alloula, Malek. *The Colonial Harem.* Translated by Myrna Godzich and Wlad Godzich. Minneapolis: University of Minnesota Press, 1986.

Amico, Michael. "The Forgotten Union of the Two Henrys: A History of the 'Peculiar and Rarest Intimacy' of the American Civil War." PhD diss., Yale University, 2017.

Amin, Camron. *The Making of the Modern Iranian Woman: Gender, State Policy, and Popular Culture, 1865–1946.* Gainesville: University Press of Florida, 2002.

'Aqili, Baqir, ed. *Khatirat-i Haj 'Izz al-Mamalik Ardalan.* Tehran: Namak, 1993.

Arunima, G. "Bonds of Love, Ties of Kinship? Or Are There Other Ways of Imagining the Family?" *Indian Economic and Social History Review* 53, no. 3 (2016): 1–22.

Astarabadi, Bibi Khanum. *Ma'ayib al-rijal.* Accessed 17 May 2021. http://www.qajarwomen.org/en/items/904A5.html.

Baron, Beth. *Egypt as a Woman: Nationalism, Gender, and Politics.* Berkeley: University of California Press, 2005.

Baron, Beth. "The Making and Breaking of Marital Bonds in Modern Egypt." In *Women in Middle Eastern History: Shifting Boundaries in Sex and Gender*, edited by Nikki R. Keddie and Beth Baron, 275–291. New Haven, CT: Yale University Press, 1991.

Bihbihani, Simin. *Ba madaram hamrah: Zindigi-namah-'i khudnivisht.* Tehran: Sukhan, 2011.

Booth, Marilyn, ed. *Harem Histories: Envisioning Places and Living Spaces*. Durham, NC: Duke University Press, 2010.

Boym, Svetlana. *The Future of Nostalgia*. New York: Basic Books, 2001.

Bray, Alan. *The Friend*. Chicago: University of Chicago Press, 2003.

Çelik, Zeynep, and Edhem Eldem, eds. *Camera Ottomana: Photography and Modernity in the Ottoman Empire, 1840–1914*. Istanbul: Koç University Publications, 2015.

Chartier, Roger, ed. *A History of Private Life*. Vol. 3: *Passions of the Renaissance*. Translated by Arthur Goldhammer. Cambridge, MA: Harvard University Press, 1989.

Cohen, Deborah. *Family Secrets: Living with Shame from the Victorians to the Present Day*. London: Viking, 2013.

Cuno, Kenneth. *Modernizing Marriage: Family, Ideology, and Law in Nineteenth- and Early Twentieth-Century Egypt*. Syracuse, NY: Syracuse University Press, 2015.

Dashtaki-nia, Farhad, trans. *Sarguzasht-i sayeh-ha: Haftad maqaleh-yi majalleh-yi Mulla Nasr al-Din dar bareh-yi zanan va kudakan*. Tehran: Nashr-i Tarikh-i Iran, 2016.

Dawlatabadi, Sadiqeh. *Nameh-ha, nivishteh-ha, and yadha*. Edited by Mahdokht Sanati and Afsaneh Najmabadi. 3 vols. Chicago: Midland Press, 1998.

Dayani, Sheida. "Juggling Revolutionaries: A Theatrical History of Indigenous Theatre and Early Playwriting in Iran." PhD diss., New York University, 2018.

Doumani, Beshara B. *Family Life in the Ottoman Mediterranean: A Social History*. Cambridge: Cambridge University Press, 2017.

Duben, Alan, and Cem Behar. *Istanbul Households: Marriage, Family and Fertility, 1880–1940*. Cambridge: Cambridge University Press, 1991.

Elling, Rasmus Christian. "Urbanizing the Iranian Public: Text, Tehran and 1922." *Middle Eastern Studies* 55, no. 3 (2019): 301–318.

Farman Farmaian, Sattareh. *Daughter of Persia: A Woman's Journey from Her Father's Harem through the Islamic Revolution*. London: Bantam Press, 1992.

Farmanfarmayan, Mihrmah. *Zir-i nigah-i pidar: Khatirat-i Mihrmah Farmanfarmayiyan az andaruni*. Tehran: Kavir, 2004.

Fay, Mary Ann. "From Warrior Grandees to Domesticated Bourgeoisie: The Transformation of the Elite Egyptian Household into a Western-Style Nuclear Family." In *Family History in the Middle East: Household, Property, Gender*, edited by B. Doumani, 77–97. Albany: State University of New York Press, 2003.

Firouz, Shahroukh. *Dar Sayeh-i Alburz* [Under the shade of Alborz: A memoir]. Odenton, MD: Mage Persian Editions, 2011.

Furughi, Muhammad 'Ali. *Yaddashtha-yi ruzaneh*. Edited by Iraj Afshar. Tehran: Kitabkhaneh, Muzeh va Markaz-i Asnad-i Majlis-i Shawra-yi Islami, 2009.

Ghaffari, Farrukh, ed. *Mahin Banu*. Tehran: Farzan, 2001.

Goldstein, Judith. "Iranian Jewish Women's Magical Narratives." In *Discourse and the Social Life of Meaning*, edited by June R. Wyman, 147–168. Washington, DC: Smithsonian Institution Press, 1986.

Goodman, Dena. "Letter Writing and the Emergence of Gendered Subjectivity in Eighteenth-Century France." *Journal of Women's History* 17, no. 2 (Summer 2005): 9–37.

Haeri, Shahla. *Law of Desire: Temporary Marriage in Shi'i Iran*. Syracuse, NY: Syracuse University Press, 1989.

Haeri, Shahla. "Temporary Marriage: An Islamic Discourse on Female Sexuality in Iran." *Social Research* 59, no. 1 (1992): 201–223.

Hijazi, Muhammad. *Huma*. Tehran: Ibn Sina, 1960.

Hirsch, Marianne, ed. *The Familial Gaze*. Hanover, NH: University Press of New England, 1999.

Hirsch, Marianne. *Family Frames: Photography, Narrative, and Postmemory*. Cambridge, MA: Harvard University Press, 1997.

Hoskins, Janet. *Biographical Objects: How Things Tell the Stories of People's Lives*. New York: Routledge, 1998.

Ihtisham al-Dawlah, Khanlar Mirza. *Ta'dib al-nisvan*. Accessed 17 May 2021. http://www .qajarwomen.org/en/items/904A3.html.

Kandiyoti, Deniz. "Some Awkward Questions on Women and Modernity in Turkey." In *Remaking Women: Feminism and Modernity in the Middle East*, edited by Lila Abu-Lughod, 270–287. Princeton, NJ: Princeton University Press, 1998.

Karachi, Ruhangiz. "Who Is the Original Author of Ta'dib al-nisvan?" *Tarikh-i adabiyat* 65, no. 3 (2010): 199–208.

Karimi, Pamela. *Domesticity and Consumer Culture in Iran: Interior Revolutions of the Modern Era*. New York: Routledge, 2013.

Kashani-Sabet, Firoozeh. *Conceiving Citizens: Women and the Politics of Motherhood in Iran*. New York: Oxford University Press, 2011.

Kasravi, Ahmad. *Dar piramun-i adabiyat*. Tehran: Firdaus, 1999.

Khalili, 'Abbas. *Ruzgar-i siyah*, first edition, 1924. Second printing, digital edition: http:// dl.nlai.ir/UI/048a3750–094e-4996-baab-64c9b8b33a1e/LookInside.aspx; Ramadan 1343, printed by Kitabkhanah-i Kaveh, a digital copy of the fourth edition published in 1936, http://dl.nlai.ir/UI/58de8e87-ba90–43b6-ac52–9d400e7f684e/LookInside.aspx.

Kholoussy, Hanan. *For Better, for Worse: The Marriage Crisis That Made Modern Egypt*. Stanford, CA: Stanford University Press, 2010.

Kracauer, Siegfried. "Photography." Translated by Thomas Y. Levin. *Critical Inquiry* 19 (Spring 1993): 421–436.

Kuhn, Annette. *Family Secrets: Acts of Memory and Imagination*. 1995. London: Verso, 2002.

Ladieh-Fuladi, Mari. *Jam'iyyat va siyasat dar Iran: Az mashruteh ta jumhuri-yi Islami*, Tehran: Mu'asseh-i Mutali'at-i Jam'iyat Shinasi Faranseh, 2003.

Latour, Bruno. *We Have Never Been Modern*. Cambridge, MA: Harvard University Press, 1993.

Lewis, Reina. *Rethinking Orientalism: Women, Travel and the Ottoman Harem*. New Brunswick, NJ: Rutgers University Press, 2004.

Mallah, Narjis Mihrangiz. *Az zanan-i pishgam-i Irani: Afzal Vaziri, dukhtar-i Bibi Khanum Astarabadi*. Tehran: Shirazeh, 2006.

Marashi, Afshin. "Print Culture and Its Publics: A Social History of Bookstores in Tehran, 1900–1950." *International Journal of Middle East Studies* 47 (2015): 89–108.

Marcus, Sharon. *Between Women: Friendship, Desire, and Marriage in Victorian England.* Princeton, NJ: Princeton University Press, 2007.

Marefat, Mina. "Building to Power: Architecture of Tehran 1921–1941." PhD diss., MIT, 1988. https://dspace.mit.edu/handle/1721.1/14535.

Menashri, David. *Education and the Making of Modern Iran.* Ithaca, NY: Cornell University Press, 1992.

Meriwether, Margaret. *The Kin Who Count: Family and Society in Ottoman Aleppo, 1770–1840.* Austin: University of Texas Press, 1999.

Mihrabi, Mu'in al-Din. "Nigahi beh ruznameh-i *Mulla Nasr al-Din*." *Kitab-i mah*, April/May 2008, 40–47.

Miller, Nancy. "Putting Ourselves in the Picture: Memoirs and Mourning." In *The Familial Gaze*, edited by Marianne Hirsch, 51–66. Hanover, NH: University Press of New England, 1999.

Miller, Nancy K. *What They Saved: Pieces of a Jewish Past.* Lincoln: University of Nebraska Press, 2011.

Mirza'i, Muhsin, ed. *Ruznamah-i khatirat-i Ghulam'ali Khan 'Aziz al-Sultan*, 4 vols. Tehran: Zaryab, 1997.

Motamedi, Mohsen. *Jughrafiya-yi tarikhi-i Tihran.* Tehran: Markaz-i Nashr-i Danishgahi, 2002.

Motlagh, Amy. *Burying the Beloved: Marriage, Realism, and Reform in Modern Iran.* Stanford, CA: Stanford University Press, 2012.

Mu'ayyir al-Mamalik, Dust'alikhan. *Vaqayi' al-zaman: Khatirat-i shikariyah.* Edited by Khadijeh Nizam Mafi. Tehran: Nashr-i Tarikh-i Iran, 1982.

Mushfiq Kazimi, Murtiza. *Ruzgar va andishah-ha.* 2 vols. Tehran: Ibn Sina, 1973.

Mushfiq Kazimi, Murtiza. *Tihran-i makhauf.* 5th edition. Tehran: Ibn Sina, 1961.

Mushfiq Kazimi, Murtiza. *Yadigar-i yik shab.* Tehran: Ibn Sina, 1961.

Mu'tamidi, Muhsin. *Jughrafiya-yi tarikhi-i Tihran.* Tehran: Markaz-i Nashr-i Danishgahi, 2002.

Naficy, Hamid. *A Social History of Iranian Cinema.* Vol. 1: *The Artisanal Era, 1897–1941.* Durham, NC: Duke University Press, 2011.

Nafisi, Sa'id. *Khatirat-i adabi, siyasi, va javani.* Edited by 'Aliriza I'tisami. Tehran: Nashr-i Markaz, 2002.

Najmabadi, Afsaneh. *Women with Mustaches and Men without Beards: Gender and Sexual Anxieties of Iranian Modernity.* Berkeley: University of California Press, 2005.

Nashat, Guity. "Marriage in the Qajar Period." In *Women in Iran: From 1800 to the Islamic Republic*, edited by Lois Beck and Guity Nashat, 37–62. Urbana: University of Illinois Press, 2004.

Nasim-i, Shumal. *Kulliyat-i javdanah Nasim-i Shumal.* Edited by Husayn Namini. Tehran: Asatir, 1992.

Nazimi, Nazila, ed. *Sih ruz bih akhar-i darya: Safarnamah-i shahzadah khanum-i Qajari.* Tehran: Atraf, 2018.

Pedersen, Claus. *The Rise of the Persian Novel: From the Constitutional Revolution to Reza Shah, 1910–1927.* Wiesbaden: Harrassowitz Verlag, 2016.

Pérez González, Carmen. *Local Portraiture: Through the Lens of the 19th Century Iranian Photographers*. Leiden: Leiden University Press, 2012.

Perrot, Michelle, ed. *A History of Private Life*. Vol. 4: *From the Fires of Revolution to the Great War*. Translated by Arthur Goldhammer. Cambridge, MA: Harvard University Press, 1990.

Povinelli, Elizabeth A. *The Empire of Love: Toward a Theory of Intimacy, Genealogy, and Carnality*. Durham, NC: Duke University Press, 2006.

Razzaque, Arafat. "The Sin of Ghība in Early Islamic Thought: The Zuhd Tradition, Late Antique Religion, and Ibn Abī l-Dunyā's Book on the Ethics of the Tongue." PhD diss., Harvard University, 2020.

Rezvani-Naraghi, Ashkan. "Middle Class Urbanism: The Socio-spatial Transformation of Tehran, 1921–41." *Iranian Studies* 51, no. 1 (2018): 97–126.

Ringer, Monica M. *Education, Religion, and the Discourse of Cultural Reform in Qajar Iran*. Costa Mesa, CA: Mazda, 2001.

Rostam-Kolayi, Jasamin. "Expanding Agendas for the 'New' Iranian Woman: Family Law, Work, and Unveiling." In *The Making of Modern Iran: State and Society under Riza Shah, 1921–1941*, edited by Stephanie Cronin, 157–190. New York: Routledge, 2003.

Rostam-Kolayi, Jasamin. "The *Tarbiyat* Girls' School of Tehran: Iranian and American Baha'i Contributions to Modern Education." *Middle East Critique* 22, no. 1 (2013): 77–93.

Roxburgh, David J., and Mary McWilliams, eds. *Technologies of the Image: Art in 19th-Century Iran*. Cambridge, MA: Harvard Art Museums, 2017.

Salur, Qahriman Mirza 'Ayn al-Saltaneh. *Ruznamah-'i khatirat-i 'Ayn al-Saltaneh*, 10 volumes. Edited by Iraj Afshar and Mas'ud Salur. Tehran: Intisharat-i Asatir, 1995–2001.

Scheiwiller, Staci Gem. *Liminalities of Gender and Sexuality in Nineteenth-Century Iranian Photography: Desirous Bodies*. New York: Routledge, 2017.

Scheiwiller, Staci Gem. "Modern Family: The Transformation of the Family Photograph in Qajar Iran." *Family Photographs* 9, no. 1 (Fall 2018). http://hdl.handle.net/2027/spo .7977573.0009.109.

Scott, James A., John Tehranian, and Jeremy Mathias. "The Production of Legal Identities Proper to States: The Case of the Permanent Family Surname." *Comparative Studies of Society and History* 44 (2002): 4–44.

Shahri, Ja'far. *Tihran-i qadim*. Vol. 1. Tehran: Mu'in, 1991.

Shahshahani, Sohelia. *Persian Clothing during the Qajar Reign* [in Persian]. Tehran: Farhangsara-yi Mirdashti, 2008.

Shahvar, Soli. *The Forgotten Schools: The Baha'is and Modern Education in Iran, 1899–1934*. London: I. B. Tauris, 2009.

Sheehi, Stephen. *The Arab Imago: A Social History of Portrait Photography, 1860–1910*. Princeton, NJ: Princeton University Press, 2016.

Siegel, Evan. "A Woman's Letters to *Molla Nasr od-Din* (Tiflis)." In *Presse und Öffentlichkeit im Nahen Östen*, edited by Christopher Herzog et al., 143–153. Heidelberg: Heidelberg Orientverlag, 1995.

Simmel, Georg. "Secrecy." In *Sociology of Georg Simmel*, edited and translated by Kurt H. Wolff, 330–344. New York: Free Press, 1967.

Sreenivas, Mytheli. *Wives, Widows, Concubines: The Conjugal Family Ideal in Colonial India*. Bloomington: Indiana University Press, 2008.

Stanley, Amy. "Maidservants' Tales: Narrating Domestic and Global History in Eurasia, 1600–1900." *American Historical Review* 121, no. 2 (2016): 437–460.

Sullivan, Zohreh. *Exiled Memories: Stories of Iranian Diaspora*. Philadelphia: Temple University Press, 2001.

Tadmor, Naomi. "The Concept of the Household-Family in Eighteenth-Century England." *Past and Present* 151 (May 1996): 111–140.

Taj al-Saltaneh. *Khatirat*. Edited by Mansureh Ittihadiyeh and Cirus Sa'dvandiyan. Tehran: Nashr-i Tarikh-i Iran, 1983.

Taussig, Michael. *Defacement: Public Secrecy and the Labor of the Negative*. Stanford, CA: Stanford University Press, 1999.

Tran, Lisa. *Concubines in Court: Marriage and Monogamy in Twentieth-Century China*. Lanham, MD: Rowman and Littlefield, 2015.

Tremayne, Soraya. "Modernity and Early Marriage in Iran: A View from Within." *Journal of Middle Eastern Women's Studies* 2, no. 1 (Winter 2006): 65–94.

Tucker, Judith E. *Women in Nineteenth-Century Egypt*. Cambridge: Cambridge University Press, 1985.

Turkle, Sherry, ed. *Evocative Objects: Things We Think With*. Cambridge, MA: MIT Press, 2007.

Ulrich, Laurel. *A House Full of Females: Plural Marriage and Women's Rights in Early Mormonism, 1835–1870*. New York: Alfred A. Knopf, 2017.

Watenpaugh, Heghnar Zeitlian. "The Harem as Biography: Domestic Architecture, Gender, and Nostalgia in Modern Syria." In *Harem Histories: Envisioning Places and Living Spaces*, edited by Marilyn Booth, 211–236. Durham, NC: Duke University Press, 2010.

Yaghoobi, Claudia. *Temporary Marriage in Iran: Gender and Body Politics in Modern Iranian Film and Literature*. Cambridge: Cambridge University Press, 2020.

Yildiz, Ihsan. "Non-recognition of Post-modern Turkish Socio-legal Reality and the Predicament of Women." *British Journal of Middle Eastern Studies* 30, no. 1 (2003): 25–41.

Zanjani, Shaykh Ibrahim. *Khatirat-i Shaykh Ibrahim Zanjani: Sar'guzasht-i zindagani-i man*. Edited by Ghulamhusayn Mirza Salih. Tehran: Kavir, 2001.

INDEX

Banu. *See* Nisa', Hajieh

bath time, families, 124

Batul Khanum, 128

Bayat, Behrouz, 71

Bayat, Muhammad Zaman, 138n74

Behar, Cem, 57

bigamy, xiii, 1, 24, 77, 88, 95, 106; falling out of favor, 78; law cartoon, 35; shame and, 34–37

Bihbihani, Simin, 14, 113

birunis (outer quarters), 97–98, 108; with elite men, 116–117; with urban transformations, 115–117

Boym, Svetlana, 19, 59

Bray, Alan, 139n12

bureaucratization of state, in Qajar period, 116

camera, 67

Changizi, Nusrat Allah, 71

character, storytelling as historian and, 7–11

children: being tutored, 72; divorce and, 86; education for, 125–126; in joint households, 121–122, 124; marriages and, 75; with naming kin, 127–130; second marriages and, 84, 87–88; with secret kin, 112; sigheh marriages and, 87–88, 93–95, 129, 142n12

China, concubinage and, 142n19

class: elite, 115–117, 141n10; marriages and changes across, 96–110; second marriages, children and, 84; sigheh marriages and, 77–78, 82–83; urban transformations and, 111, 115

Cohen, Deborah, 2

"Concept of the Household-Family in Eighteenth-Century England, The" (Tadmor), 141n4

concubinage, 75; China and, 142n19; polygyny and, 16

conjugalization: of couples, 42–43, 60–61, 69–71; of family, xiv, 15–16, 19–20, 33, 39, 66, 68, 70, 74, 111; marriage and, 15, 28, 32, 34, 43, 45; monogamy and, 31, 33

contextualization, historians with, 9–10

cookbook, 53–54

Corbin, Alain, 9

couples: conjugalization of, 42–43, 60–61, 69–71; family photographs of married, 69–70

culture: with family and marrying for love, 13–15, 23–24; "Print Culture and Its Publics," 146n14; street strolling, 117–120

Cuno, Kenneth, 66

Dabir al-Sultan, 96

Dar al-Funun, 116

Dargahi, Kaukab, 82

Dark days (*Ruzgar-i siyah*) (Khalili), 23–24, 26, 86, 88, 134n28

Davud al-Saltaneh, 99, 125, 129

Dawlatabadi, Fakhr, 129

Dawlatabadi, Haj Mirza Hadi, 129

Dawlatabadi, Qamar, 129

Dawlatabadi, Sadiqeh, 81, 129, 143n24, 148n11

Dawlatshahi, Zahra Malik, 106

Dayani, Sheida, 26–27

Defense Lawyers, The (Akhundzadeh), 27

diaries, memoirs and, 118

Disciplining Women (Ihtisham al-Dawlah), 28, 136n44

divorce: stigma of, 85–86; women and, 143n24

dress, wedding: European-style white, 60, 62, 64–65; Naqdah, 63; of Qahrimani, 61

Duben, Alan, 57

education, 145n9; for children, 125–126; higher learning, 116; of men, 29; of women, 23–24, 26–29, 45, 74, 89, 125

Egypt, 68

elite class, 115–117, 141n10

Elizabeth II (Queen of England), 67

ethics: of marriage, 75; of speech, 3; of stories not meant for retelling, 1–6

Europeans: moral corruption of, 77; with white wedding dresses, 60, 62, 64–65; wives, 81

extended family, 132n11

Fakhr al-Dawleh, 44

Fakhr al-Muluk, 44, 48

Fakhr al-Saltaneh, 138n7

family: ahl-i manzil and, 76; aristocratic, 60; arranged marriages, Qajar period and, 20–21; bath time, 124; conjugalization of, xiv, 15–16, 19–20, 33, 39, 66, 68, 70, 74, 111;

criticism of, 27; with culture and marrying for love, 13–15, 23–24; evolution of, 15; extended, 132n11; household-, 76, 132n11, 141n4; joint households, 100–104, 120–126; law reform, 27; letters, xiv, 41–57; Mallah, 71, 73, 90; marriages with evolution of, xiv; marriage with love over, 24; with naming marriage and kin, 127–130; with nuclear or more complex structures, 17; with ordinary objects of life, xiv, 59; practices and generational changes, 89–95; sigheh marriages and, 81–83, 89; urban transformations with secret, xiv–xv; Vaziri/Mallah, 89–95; wedding outfits and studio photographs, xiv, 57–66

family photographs: conjugalization and, xiv, 68, 70; hallway leading to yard, 114; Khanum Afzal in, 71, 72, 74; Mallah, 71, 73–74; with marriage and meanings, 85, 93, 99, 104–105; married couples, 69–70; oral stories and, 67–68; role of, 140n34; WWQI digital archives with, 68

Farah al-Saltaneh, 43

farang (marital relations of Europeans), 28–31, 146n10

Farge, Arlette, 8–9

Fari (mother), xii, 1, 2; cookbook of, 53, 54; joint households and, 102–103, 124, 126–127; letters from 'Abbas to, 43, 44, 47–57, 52, 58; marrying for love, 13, 14, 18; naming kin, 127; nursing instruction book, 53, 55; suitors warded off by, 14; with urban transformations, 114; wedding dress of, 60, 62, 66; wedding memories, 62; wedding photograph of 'Abbas and, 65

Farinaz, 51, 103, 113

Farmanfarma household, 28–29, 60, 127–129, 144n48

Farmanfarmayan, Mihrmah, 28–29, 60, 64, 85–86, 127–129, 146n10

Fate's Spring, The (film), 137n60

Fatih, Salar, 84

Fatimah Sultan, 106

Fatimeh, 87–88

Fatimeh (Khanum jun), 87–88

fiction. See novels

Firuz, Maryam, 28

Friend, The (Bray), 139n12

friendship: letters and, 46–47; love, affection, and, 30–32, 42–43

Furughi, Muhammad 'Ali, 118

Galin Baji, 106

gardens, 119

Gawhar al-Muluk, 48, 121, 125, 129

genealogy: of Badi' al-Saltaneh, 98; fragment, 94; of Vaziri/Mallah family, 90

Ghaffari, Farrukh, 120, 128, 130

Ghanoonparvar, M., 21, 24

Gheissari, Ali, 115

Ghosh, Amitav, 11

Giti Afruz, 14, 33, 137nn59–61

Goldstein, Judith, 111

Goodman, Dena, 46–47

gossip: with circulation network disrupted, 112–113; disavowal of, 3, 36; key players, 113; rumor and, 9; secrets and, 145n4; as source of knowledge, 3, 8

Gul-i zard (newspaper), 135n42

Hadi, Kal, 60

Hadi, Ma'sumeh, 60

Haeri, Shahla, 34

Haji Nasir al-Saltaneh Diba, 41

Haj Mahmud Mu'tamad al-Sultan, 89

Halimeh Khanum, 84–85

Hasanabad residential complex: inner quarters, 97–98, 122; mini-bazaar and, 121; outer quarters, 97–98; as rebuilt in 1964, 123; as refurbished in 2000, 123; urban transformation and, 115, 121–123

Hazrat, Sadiq, 118

Heart's targets (Amaj-i dil) (Vafa), 48

Heripsima, 69

hijab, 14, 124–125

Hijazi, Muhammad, 21, 24–26, 32, 134n25, 134n30

Hisam al-Dawleh, 44–45

historians: motivations of, 2; on nostalgia, 19; role of, 8–10; storytelling as character and, 7–11

historicism, 9

homes, urban transformations of, 115–120

honor-killing, 27–28

Hoskins, Janet, 67

Saʻi, Karim, 49, 141n7
Sakineh Khanum, 43, 106
sales, map of, 101
satire, marrying for love and, 26–28
secrets: benefits of, 2; around bigamy, 34; families and urban transformations, xiv–xv; gossip and, 145n4; kin, 112; marriages, 87–89; second families and, xi–xv; sigheh marriages as, 34–39, 81, 91–92
servant, in gossip network, 113
sexually forbidden, with broken trust, 84
sexual monogamy, 31, 33, 137n56
sexual pleasure: procreation and, 75, 77; sigheh marriages and, 77–78, 81
Shahroukh, Firouz, 146n10
Shahshahani, Sohelia, 60
Shahzadeh Baygum, 109
Shahzadeh Khanum Kuch, 43
Shajan. See Malik, Zahra
shame, bigamy and, 34–37
Shams al-Muluk, 44–46
Shams al-Muluk Azudi, 42–44, 138n1
Shams al-Muluk Jahanbani, 62
Shams al-Saltaneh, 136n52, 138n9
Shams al-Taj, 108
Shargh (newspaper), 35
Shaykh ʻAbbas, 87–88
Shaykh al-Islam, 43
Shazdeh Baygum Khanum (Mufarrah al-Dawleh), 82
Shazdeh Muluk, 84, 89
sigheh marriages, 75; children and, 87–88, 93–95, 129, 142n12; class and, 77–78, 82–83; connotations, 133n17; family and, 81–83, 89; men and, xiv; prostitution and, 16, 34; as secret, 34–39, 81, 91–92; sexual pleasure and, 77–78, 81
silent strike, against second marriage, 83–84
Simmel, Georg, 112, 145n4
Sirishk (Hijazi), 24
Siyahatnamah-i Ibrahim Bayg, 20
skirt, velvet embroidery wedding, 60, 62
slavery, polygyny and, 16
speech, ethics of, 3
Stanley, Amy, 28
state business, offices for, 116
status groups. See class
storytelling: as character and historian, 7–11;

ethics and stories not meant for retelling, 1–6; with gossip disavowed, 3
streets, urban transformations of, 115–120
street strolling culture, 117–120
strikes: marital, 100; silent, 83–84
studio photographs, wedding outfits and, xiv, 57–66
Suez (film), 137n60
Suhrab al-Saltaneh, 99
suitors, warding off, 14, 77
Sulayman Khan, 109
Surur al-Saltaneh, 30–32, 41, 43–45, 136n52

Tabrizi, Mirza Aqa, 27–28
Tadmor, Naomi, 76, 132n11, 141n4
Taj al-Saltaneh, 28, 78
Talibuf, 20
Tarbiyat (newspaper), 118
Tarbiyat School for Girls and Zhandark, 28, 29, 136n47
Tayeh Khanum, 113
Taymurtash (ʻAbd al-Husayn Muʻazzaz al-Mulk), 136n52, 138n1, 138n9, 141nn10–11; early years, 29; letters from early in marriage, 44–46; on love, friendship, and affection, 32; with love letters and language, 30–31, 41; with Markariyan, 80–81
Tehran: population, 111–112; Ramadan and, 115; school locations on map, 126; with urban transformations, 114
Tehrani, Yusif Jalili, 64
Tihran-i makhauf (Kazimi), 22–26, 32, 88, 134n27
Tran, Lisa, 142n19
trust, sexually forbidden with broken, 84
Turkey, 68
Turkle, Sherry, 67

Ulrich, Laurel, 67
urban transformations: with affective life of joint households, 100–104, 120–126; class and, 111, 115; family photo with hallway leading to yard, 114; Hasanabad residential complex and, 115, 121–123; of home and streets, 115–120; with house size and architecture changing, 111–114; inner quarters and, 115, 116, 122; monogamy and, 111;